Healing Journeys
How Trauma Survivors
Learn to Live Again

Healing Journeys

How Trauma Survivors Learn to Live Again

Linda Daniels, Psy.D.

New Horizon Press
Far Hills, New Jersey

Linda Daniels, Psy.D.
    Healing Journeys: How Trauma Survivors
    Learn to Live Again

Cover Design: Bob Aulicino
Interior Design: Susan Sanderson

Library of Congress Control Number: 2003105790

ISBN: 0-88282-239-X
New Horizon Press

Manufactured in the U.S.A.

2007   2006   2005   2004   2003   /   5   4   3   2   1

Table of Contents

Heart of the City

You can tear down a building
You can tear down a park
You can strike at a symbol
But you can't touch the heart

- Janis Ian

Introduction

Traumatic events—fatal accidents, serious injuries, violent crimes, plane crashes and earthquakes—are all, sadly, universal phenomena. Regardless of origin, however, each trauma experienced is an event that can be singularly devastating to the emotions, mind and heart of an individual. That the event occurred, that it was horrific in its scope and that there was a great personal loss or a perceived threat of violence or death is the crux of any experience of trauma.

In the chapters which follow you will read about individuals who have felt the initial impact of trauma and suffered the consequent helplessness, shock, fear and grief. Perhaps, since you have chosen to read this book these will be familiar feelings. You will begin a journey of healing and recovery with a varied selection of these survivors. As you will discover on these journeys, "closure," for some survivors, is a moot point. Hopefully, though, you will begin to realize that more important than the use of a term that many survivors find empty, is the resilience—the rising of the human spirit—in the face of devastating life events. Many of the survivors whose stories you will read gave gained such resilience.

The trauma survivors from whom you will hear are mothers, fathers, sisters, brothers, cousins, uncles, aunts, grandparents and friends. They come from all walks of life. They are executives, food service workers, laborers, secretaries and supervisors. You will find that their individual paths to healing are rich with the various cultures, beliefs, values and socio-economic dimensions that characterize diversity. In the process of becoming witness to their experiences as they attend to their day-to-day activities and work towards healing, I hope you will find in their experiences, struggles and exercises techniques to employ in your own process of healing.

As you progress on your own journey, you will gain a greater understanding of trauma, both obvious and subtle. Where these survivors found themselves at the embarkation point of their healing will help define common stages of trauma; where they are years later will demonstrate each survivor's unique path to healing. And where they seem to be heading in the future may shed further light for you not only on their struggles, resilience and self-growth, but your own. Ultimately, as you follow these survivors on their journey from horror to life-affirming renewal and hope, their journeys will you in your own life.

The extraordinary process of healing and recovery from a traumatic event is a journey with which I empathize and which I share. A licensed psychologist and board-certified trauma expert, I too am a survivor. I was working on the 62nd floor of the World Trade Center during the September 11, 2001 terrorist attack. I understand intimately this passage to healing from my own personal experience. Though people in many lands throughout the world have seen and felt trauma in their own countries, grievous, intentional violence against people on American soil has occurred with such catastrophic force only on few occasions: the War of 1812, the American Civil War, the Japanese attacks on the American naval base at Pearl Harbor and the World Trade Center attacks in 1993 and in 2001. The annihilation of the innocent on September 11, 2001 emotionally touched people everywhere, but especially impacted Americans' view of their own and their country's safety.

On the afternoon of that tragic day, I received a call from the major metropolitan transportation agency where I had been working that morning. I was asked to establish and direct a trauma crisis center the following morning. For the next three months, I managed over 150 volunteer mental health professionals, nurses and clergy: people who gave freely and fully of their skills, time and energy. These clinicians heard many painful and poignant stories of survival, heart-wrenching accounts from witnesses of horrific death and of last conversations with missing loved ones. Shock, fear, uncertainty, horror and terror—the list of emotions experienced by trauma survivors was long and painful. And I knew from past experience with those touched by tragedy that the more intimate the survivor's relationship to trauma, the more devastating it can be to the spirit.

Since the World Trade Center attacks, I have maintained contact with more than two hundred survivors and have helped guide many on their paths to healing. It is gratifying to see that many survivors are continuing onward toward emotional health, showing admirable resilience in the face of the catastrophic series of events that occurred on that tragic day and the adverse emotional rippling effects that followed. Over the years, I also have treated survivors of other traumatic incidents—those who survived incest, physical injury, the murder or accidental death of loved ones and many other life-altering events. For any trauma survivor, past, present or future, the ultimate challenge always is to persevere emotionally in the face of horrendous experience no matter how or when it occurs.

By sharing experiences from some of the trauma survivors I have treated in my capacity as a psychologist and those I have counseled and guided following September 11th, as well as my own experiences, I want to help those who still struggle with feelings of despair. It is also my hope that the lessons I have learned along my own journey will assist my professional colleagues to better help others who are trying to cope with trauma.

I now know intimately that grief and loss resulting from traumatic events stab the soul like a dagger. It leaves the self initially stunned, sometimes unable to comprehend the largest dimension or the most minute details of the event's details. Then, like a flood, the magnitude of the event's essence rushes in, shocking the physical self and the mind. Emotional waves swell and assail the psyche, leaving the body feeling like a battered shell that has lost part of itself, its spirit. The human spirit often fights hard against such attacks and then ebbs against a tide of rising despair, emotional peaks and lows often typifying its pattern. Still, the human spirit can rise up against this assault and begin to reclaim itself. It is reassuring to be aware that though sometimes the spirit retreats altogether for a period of time, it often returns renewed, stronger and more resilient than ever.

To you who suffer I offer encouragement in my own words and those of other survivors; first, to reassure all of you who are enduring the ordeals, emotions and confrontations of the stages of trauma, including those I have treated in my private practice and those who survived the September 11th terrorist attacks. Trauma affects us all in dramatic ways. However, as you will find as you read on, many survivors have searched out and found ways not only to cope successfully but also to regain hope. As a survivor myself, I know that there is great solace in this fact. As the survivors you will meet in the following pages describe their healing processes, they offer coping tools as diverse as the people describing them.

I hope their messages and mine will bring you comfort and support as you journey on.

Chapter 1

My Trauma Revisited

There are few times in life when the frailty of our existence and the fortitude of the human spirit make themselves known simultaneously. We rise each morning and unconsciously rely on the control we believe we exert on the world. We have faith that what we do, say and think are guarantees of what is to be. Then, in seconds, life unceremoniously knocks us on the seat of our pants.

For me, September 11, 2001 started like the day before it and the day before that. The only difference I could discern as I remember the beginning of that day after I arrived at my office was that it was an exceptionally warm, clear-skied beautiful Tuesday morning. But then,

What the... I thought in confusion, the intercom phone frozen midway between its cradle and my ear, as I stared incredulously out my office window on the 62nd floor of One World Trade Center watching objects falling down: large chunks of concrete, shattered debris, unidentifiable steel. (Only later did I allow myself to acknowledge that human bodies and body parts were just as much a part of these images that would be forever encoded in my mind's eye.) As I stood trying to make sense of the debris plummeting just outside my window, the building tilted at what felt like a 45-degree angle. Leaving everything behind, I rushed to the reception area. In the split second that it took to look upon the near paralysis of the people gathered in the waiting room, pure fear gripped me. More than twelve people stood there, their arms spread out as if to protect their personal space, their minds, it seemed, desperately trying to gauge the enormity of the unthinkable. Then, the seconds began to swim by in a time warp identifiable only in hindsight. "Get out!" someone yelled as the building lunged again, swaying back and forth, back and forth.

I ran to the nearest stairwell, fueled by my body's adrenaline and a sense of doom I had never before experienced. I began racing down the stairs with all the speed inside me, at times falling only to immediately pick myself up with little break in my stride. The rational part of me screamed, "Take off your shoes! Take off your shoes!" At first I just could not comprehend the command, then I unceremoniously dismissed it. I can't waste a second, I thought. Only after falling for the third or fourth time, with absolute trepidation, did I pause long enough to slide my shoes off my feet before starting to run again at full speed, holding my shoes like batons in a relay race, while the heavy footsteps of others pounded above me. In an instant I was overcome with a sense of terror and indescribable fear; the possibility of death became razor sharp real and pervaded me. Despite the thousands of people that I knew were in the building, I felt utterly alone.

Then calmness took over. Those who know me typically describe me as calm, usually undaunted by even the most challenging situation. Yet, I knew, in the midst of such a terrifying unknown, my outward calm was only a wedge against my fear, a fear that threatened to consume me as I suddenly felt cramped in a stairwell that was rapidly feeling smaller and smaller. Almost instantaneously, I became acutely aware that at every third floor or so, a "No re-entry" sign seemed to mock me, letting me know that even though I could enter the stairwell, given the split second between life and death, I could not exit to survival. *I don't want to die like this.* Such thoughts propelled me toward a growing panic. As my heart began to race, I fought to choke down the anxiety, deeply inhaling the air around me. In that moment I vowed to myself that I would at least continue to "act calm" because at some instinctual level I knew that the act might serve as my lifeline for thinking clearly to at least get through the terror physically intact.

By the time I reached the twenty-fifth floor, firefighters, decked out in full rescue gear, were ascending the stairs.

"It gets a little smoky as you go down, but it's not unbearable. Just continue to remain calm. You're safe now," one fireman said reassuringly.

Near the 20th floor, voices above me began shouting "We have a burn victim! We have a burn victim!"

Without hesitation, hundreds of people in the stairwell moved aside as a woman who appeared to be in her thirties slowly made her way past, seeming to almost float down the steps. As she passed me I saw that she was burned on every visible part of her body. She looked to be in severe shock; her eyes held a far-away, glazed look. With what looked like a half-smile, her expression was beyond description.

I lost track of time and location. A chant began to play in my head, *Step down, step down, step down.* Near the eighth floor, the stairs became slippery with water and the smoke heavier in the air. The tension of others around me began to mount. No longer chatting nervously, people moved quickly, with a sense of heightened urgency and purpose.

At last we were nearing the final landing. "There it is," I said with relief.

We stepped on to the concourse floor.

War Zone! my mind roared. Boulder-like chunks of concrete peppered the building's lobby floor. The elevator doors were blackened. "What could have caused so much damage all the way down here?" I wondered as I moved sideways through twisted mangled revolving doors toward the concourse shopping area. Fire sprinklers drenched us; broken glass crunched underfoot; feet bled. I looked in bewilderment at the utter destruction around me. Yet, as I took in the devastation around me, something else nagged at me. I kept telling myself that there was something I was missing. Finally, my amorphous thoughts clicked into place, as if on a rusty chain. *The elevators*! I thought, as I remembered the blackened, deformed elevator doors and suddenly understood the portentous implications. Oh my God. *Who was inside the elevators when this all began? Could there have been people I knew inside?* My mind created a hideous scenario: the elevators free-falling forty-four floors to the concourse level. Images of mangled bodies leaked into my mind like poison. With great effort, I pulled myself back to the present, trying to regain my focus on what I needed to do to survive as hundreds of us were being herded toward an escalator that stood between the street level entrance of a bookstore and an ATM machine on Church Street.

With the devastation of the concourse before me, my survival instincts were on overload and the adrenaline coursed feverishly through my body.

We finally made it through the double doors, out of the building, and on to the street.

Oh my God, oh my God, I thought as I looked up and saw, for the first time, the blackened, smoldering hole that was the top floors of the tower I had just escaped, the tall antenna that usually stood atop no longer visible to me.

Oh my God, Oh my God, oh my God, oh my God became a mantra in my head as it slowly dawned on me that the second building also had a smoldering, gaping hole through many of its floors, with black smoke and flames defiantly pouring out. More than an hour had passed between the moment the plane struck One World Trade Center, the North Tower, and the instant that thousands had shakily but safely escaped from the building. And in that time period (my mind propelling me to the obvious conclusion) Two World Trade Center had also been struck. I stared at the cataclysmic horror in disbelief.

Oh my God, we're being attacked! my brain screamed. I was still unable to speak

I stood there, rooted and helpless, as a steady stream of people walked past me, many with hollow, dazed eyes. Others were sobbing hysterically and still others were physically supporting friends. I looked up again. Black Smoke. Flames. Devastation. Destruction. Unbidden, the chant in my mind began again, *Oh my God, oh my God, oh my God, oh my God.*

Suddenly, a thunderous noise erupted behind me.

Dear God, another plane hit the building again! I thought.

Everyone bolted, running away from the noise. Dust chased us. The mammoth sound appeared endless and seemed to announce by its sheer volume just how truly small and fragile my life was against its magnitude. I glanced back apprehensively to make sure I was outrunning the terror that was in pursuit. The sight of dust and flying debris was made more terrifying by the thunderous sounds coming from within the cyclone-like mass, eclipsing everything surrounding and behind it.

"The building is collapsing!" someone shrieked.

I continued to run at full speed. For long moments, only screams filled the air, blocking out everything else. I could no longer hear the whining of the police sirens or the praying of others.

I allowed myself another look behind.

Where is the building? It's gone! Oh my God. The building is gone! I continued to run.

Blocks later, I jumped inside a taxicab with four strangers.

"Who wants to try my phone?" one of them asked.

I tried to reach my mother at work. I tried my best friend. No luck. Next, I dialed my grandmother's telephone number and heard the line ringing. "Oh, good, I got through!" I thought gratefully as my grandmother answered.

"Hi, Grandma," I said, feeling suddenly drained as if I could finally lay down my fear, knowing my grandmother would help share the heavy load.

"Oh Lord, I'm so happy to hear your voice," she cried. "Oh Linda, we were so scared. Your mother has been calling every two seconds asking whether you called."

"I'm okay, Grandma," I told her.

"Thank God you're okay. God saved you. God blessed you."

She was now sobbing. Through her tears, she asked, "How could they do this? Those poor people, those poor innocent people." As she cried profusely, I heard the hysteria rising in her voice and moved to still her.

"Please try to calm down. I don't want you to get sick, Grandma."

I paused to allow her to catch her breath.

"You're the first person I've been able to reach. Can you try to call everybody and tell them that I'm okay?" I asked.

"I have to go now," I said. "Other people need to use the phone. I'll call back when I can."

I passed the telephone to the woman next to me, momentarily lost in my own thoughts about how my family and partner must be suffering tremendously with the fear of not knowing whether I was dead or alive.

The cell phone went out of service again.

Moments later rumbling noises erupted behind us again. *How much more can we take?* I thought, as our necks collectively craned toward the back window of the taxicab. In stunned horror, we watched the Tower I had escaped come crumbling down.

"They're both down!" a woman screamed. "There is no hope." She was inconsolable. The rest of us were silent.

I pulled my eyes away from the crumbling building, glancing out the passenger window. My eyes recorded everything before me: people congregated on corners, some standing in the middle of the street, slack-jawed, as they stared at the spot where the buildings once stood. In the middle of one city block, a middle-aged man in construction clothes stood on the topmost hood of a battered van. His face was raised to the sky as he sobbed with indescribable pain, exposed for the world to see. As we drove slowly past, people around him seemed oblivious to his anguish, lost in their own terror.

I need to get home right now! I said to myself as I got out of the slow-moving taxi.

I headed toward 7th Avenue and 34th Street, intent on taking the train from Pennsylvania Station to my home. Throngs of people were gathered outside the station. All service had been suspended. *Now what?* I wondered as I leaned against the building. Getting out of Manhattan had become my only goal—survival, pure and uncomplicated. I stood in front of the station, my clothes wet and dirty with dust while tears streamed down my face. I felt a sense of folding into myself as I swayed between states of semi-shock and intense reality. For a long moment, I felt completely defeated.

I took a deep breath.

"I'll walk," I said aloud and with resolve.

As I walked east, I overheard someone say, "People are crossing the Queensborough/Fifty-ninth Street Bridge."

"Yes," I exclaimed.

I headed purposefully toward the bridge, then my steps faltered as I recalled rumors that our terror might only be beginning; hijacked planes were said to be still in the air. My eyes looked upward, more than half-expecting to see death's approach.

I felt utterly under siege.

Feeling as if I had no other option, I walked across the bridge, slowly making my way among the myriad of people in front, behind and to each side of me. A half-hour later I stepped into Queens County, New York.

Within minutes a bus arrived, packed with people. I squeezed in, getting no further than the coin box bolted down next to the bus driver. As we slowly made our way through Queens, people talked about the attacks, expressing shock, disbelief and fear. My energy and focus intent only on getting home, I consciously blocked out the conversations buzzing around me.

Finally, Main Street was just a few blocks away. I got off the bus and began to walk farther east on Northern Boulevard, my apartment still more than twenty blocks away. I walked briskly but felt spacey, as if drugged. When I finally reached my apartment, I saw my landlord standing next to the house's garage. With no keys, I had already prepared to break into my own apartment. Do you have keys to my apartment with you?" I asked him.

He reached for his key chain, trying several keys before finding mine. I quickly thanked him and escaped into my apartment.

I shed my dirty, dusty clothes and sat on the living room couch, sitting very still, feeling numb, detached. Ten, then twenty minutes ticked slowly by. Finally, I got up. As I walked toward the kitchen for a glass of water, I saw that my answering machine light was blinking. I hit play and was bombarded by my mother's voice. She was apparently talking to someone with her in her Manhattan office.

"She's not there. She's not there, she's not…" my mother sobbed, hanging up the telephone mid-sentence.

The next call was from my very dearest friend.

Pleading, she said, "Tell me you took today off. Please tell me you didn't go in today." Pause. "I'm on my way." Click.

I sat down on the couch again. Stunned. More minutes passed. I got up again and picked up the telephone to call my mother. I couldn't get through. I tried to reach my grand-mother again. No luck. I then turned on the television and watched the horror unfold over and over again.

My closest friend arrived several hours later and we hugged for a long, long time, both crying in relief because I was alive and in grief because so many others were not.

Reactions to Trauma

Thankfully, I survived. Yet I had spent the entire day on emotional overload, in moments shutting down for the sake of self-preservation as the shock of the event caused my senses to weave in and out of consciousness. One moment I was acutely aware of all that was unfolding before me and in the next moment I was dazed and detached from the bombardment to my senses. My emotions were raw and overwhelming. Too much had happened on that day, a day that for myself and many others started out so ordinarily. And like survivors of any trauma, as the day came to an end, shock and helplessness were the emotions that prevailed. Similarly, yet uniquely, other survivors of the terrorist attack expressed their own memories of that day in a singular and eloquent ways. Together, these and other trauma accounts that follow provide personalized snapshots of the possible range of actions, thoughts and behaviors experienced while in the midst of a life-altering event.

Liz, a fifty-five-year-old married mother of four and grand-mother of seven who enjoys gardening and sewing, recalls:

I arrived at work at approximately 7:30 A.M. and took two banks of elevators to my office. I immediately began to gather orientation materials because I was expecting a new employee to begin her first day of work in the office. She arrived at approximately 8:40. I told her to get settled in, grab some coffee and I would meet with her in a few minutes. At 8:46 A.M., the building was suddenly struck by something. I heard a loud explosion and felt the building actually sway. I looked out of the office window and saw a big cloud of smoke, like something on fire. I went to another area of the office to retrieve one of my coworkers. Another coworker was also in the area. Together we joined the others at the stairwell.

When we entered the concourse level, there was glass and pools of blood everywhere. There was also a terrible odor that I could not name. The floor was slippery with water and I was afraid that I would cut my feet as both my coworker and myself, along with many other women, had discarded our shoes while in the stairwell in order to keep pace with the others. Ten minutes after we got out of the building, the South Tower collapsed.

I was lucky to escape the debris, but I could not escape the tremendous plume of dust that enveloped everything in its path, causing total darkness. One minute we stood against a bright day and the next moment everything turned so dark. I was gasping, choking for air, unable to see through the dust and other substances that minutes before were the material that gave form to the building in which I spent over twenty years of my working life.

I was trying to outrun the cloud of dust when suddenly it felt like someone punched me squarely in the back. That someone, out of the darkness, clutched his arm around my neck, choking me. I felt his breath against my ear as he screamed, "Please help. I don't want to die."

Feeling helpless, I thought, "Lord, just take me. If you take me now, I am ready, but please take care of my family."

As I prayed, I lost my balance and fell to the ground. I started crawling and quickly became disoriented. Eventually, with scraped knees, I tried to stand. Yet I couldn't see because dust and debris filled and burned my eyes, nose and throat.

Out of the darkness, I heard a voice saying, "Come this way." Two men pulled me into an office building that had a restaurant in its lobby. Fifteen minutes later, someone screamed that the North Tower was collapsing.

"Run away from the building!" someone yelled. I felt numb, like everything was happening to someone else.

I ran two blocks, entered another building and found myself in what looked like a shelter converted into a triage station. I sat in the shelter for some time and eventually struck up a conversation with two wonderful women. Approximately two hours later we decided to walk, for what felt like miles, to a bus stop that we hoped would eventually get us home. Together, we finally boarded a bus that took us to the George Washington Bridge Bus Terminal.

When we arrived at the terminal we were dismayed to see that there were blocks upon blocks of people waiting to get on buses into New Jersey. While standing in line I saw two transportation agency employees I knew. They took my two new friends and me out of the line and into the terminal. We went upstairs past a suite of offices and into a shower area. These kind souls then gave us clean clothes and called my husband. It was 6 P.M. and this would be my first contact with him. Because the area was in full lockdown, these great people made arrangements for me to stay overnight at a hotel in Fort Lee, New Jersey. They gave me food and helped make arrangements for my husband to gain clearance to take me home the next morning.

I shared the hotel room with three other survivors. The

entire evening I sat in a fog, confused. I watched no television nor did I listen to the radio. I sat in a chair and looked out the window. I sat in that chair the entire night and prayed to God that nothing else happened as I watched the others sleep.

As Liz came out of her trauma, fear, confusion and helplessness were her primary emotions. Over time, Liz would come to realize that she would need to come to terms with these and other disabling emotions she came to feel in the aftermath of her ordeal.

Brandon, a thirty-two-year-old father of two young children, husband and avid hunter who also enjoys fishing and sports, recounts the events of that day:

About five blocks from the site, a wave of people began walking toward us. Every one of their faces seemed to carry an unimaginable story of near-death experience. I myself was numb and in shock and everything seemed to be happening in slow motion. I remembered clearly how silent everything seemed despite all that was going on around me. It felt like being outside when sound becomes muffled by recent snowfall. And as debris fell from the building it looked like it would gently glide down without a sound. But then you heard the thuds—debris and bodies hitting the ground. One of the worst feelings was not knowing how far away was safe.

Late that afternoon, while back at my office, I remembered getting up from my chair and feeling dizzy. I didn't feel as if I was going to pass out, but more like I was frozen on the outside. I felt like my body couldn't keep up with what my mind was telling it. As I drove home that evening, the further away I got from the area, the safer I began to feel. But, at the same time, the more relaxed I seemed to feel, the less in touch I became with what was going on around me.

During his ordeal, Brandon was on emotional overload. In the aftermath of his trauma, Brandon found himself struggling to regain his life's purpose. Like many others, his trauma forced him to search deep inside himself in order to rediscover how this tragedy redefined his values.

Shock, terror, numbness and helplessness are only a few of the universal reactions we all experience when trauma confronts us. Each individual reacts in their own way to the deluge of response to such harsh events. Just as important as what happens to each person is how a trauma is experienced and the impact of its intensity. We place value on events in our lives and it is this value and how we subsequently reexperience an event that defines the impact of the trauma we feel. Like all trauma survivors, these survivors of the World Trade Center attack also would have to come to grips with the overpowering emotions unleashed in the aftermath of this tragedy.

Trauma's Many Faces

Trauma appears in many guises, as hundreds of events can evoke traumatic reactions. These events span the range of human experience and are as far-reaching as the onset of a chronic illness to automobile accidents, natural disasters, rape and murder.

For instance, trauma seems to cut through the heart of those who outlive spouses, children or other loved ones who lose their lives due to accident, violence or illness. As Janet, a twenty-two-year-old who lost her father during a robbery that led to his murder when she was ten years old, recalls:

> I remember that it was a warm day and I was playing outside with my friends. We had been running around all day and I was hot. I decided to go home to get something to drink. When I walked in the house, I immediately felt that something was wrong. My mom was crying and my grandmother was on the telephone. I asked my mother what was the matter and she told me that my father had been robbed and was in the hospital in a coma. I later learned that the men who robbed him beat him over the head with a lead pipe, crushing his skull. She told me that she would be going to the hospital right away and promised to take me the following day.

> I didn't know how to feel at the time, but I recall running

out of the house as if I was mad at someone. Somehow, I knew he was going to die and he did.

The sudden, untimely death of a loved one creates a prevailing wound to the hearts and spirits of those left to cope with such a loss. Like many who experience the unexpected death of a loved one, Janet set out on her healing journey in order to overcome the sense of unfairness, tremendous sadness, anger and the other dominating emotions which flooded her.

Just as the death of a loved one devastates, so too can the unexpectedness of physical injury. For, among its other painful consequences, physical injury often brings its survivor face to face with his or her own mortality. Bob, a forty-nine-year-old married banking executive with a twelve-year-old son, shares his story.

It was supposed to be a routine medical procedure. The nurse told me that the procedure would be done in the office and should be completed in less than an hour. Well, the next day I woke in a hospital room. They told me that there had been an accident during the procedure—my esophagus had been punctured. How could a routine procedure go so terribly wrong? I wondered if I had almost died.

I was kept in the hospital for a week. I lay in bed feeling shocked and numb the entire time. I felt like I was outside my body. I remember watching the nurses change my I.V., and I recall looking at the doctor as he spoke to me. But I was not really absorbing what he said. I just could not get past one question: "How did this happen??"

Those confronted with unexpected physical limitation often speak of suddenly feeling physically incomplete and damaged. Like others before him, Bob struggled with these and other prevailing emotions in order to heal and feel complete again.

On the whole, the impact of trauma on people can be painfully diverse and varied. As for me, later that evening on September 11th, I received a call from a client agency, requesting that I establish and direct a crisis-counseling center at a New York City airport for their employees and employee family members. I hesitated. *Can I?* I wondered. I was told that a car could be sent for me in the early morning and that others would be made available to assist me. "Okay," I finally agreed.

Shortly afterwards, I went to bed, exhausted. Somehow I had survived the worst day of my life. It was a day that would repeat itself and impinge on my life and memory in the weeks and months to follow. Along with every other survivor of trauma, I would never be the same again. Yet as the days went on, I learned, as have others who have gone before me on similarly difficult roads, that remembering and owning the experience is the first step to recovery and healing.

Chapter 1 Resilience Tips

- Healing and recovery begin with remembering and owning the entire experience.

- It is the TOTAL experience that has now been hard-wired into your mind.

- Only through fully owning your experience of the trauma can you move through its effects.

- Tell your story over and over. Tell your story verbally, in a journal or in whatever form most comfortable to you. But TELL YOUR STORY! Often, a detail, like an image or a thought to which your body and mind may be responding, evades you in the initial telling, but becomes evident as you retell your experience. What were your first thoughts? What range of emotions did you experience while present at the event? What did you see, hear and smell? How did you feel immediately afterward?

- List the full spectrum of your reactions—physical, emotional, cognitive, spiritual, etcetera.

- Know and FULLY BELIEVE that all your responses are NORMAL. To deny or dismiss your responses may prolong your suffering and protract the healing process.

- Accepting your own feelings as valid and normal is an important step to recovery.

EXERCISE

The following exercise* will help identify common post-traumatic stress reactions. For each reaction that applies to you, rate that reaction on a scale of 1 through 10 in severity.

Reaction	_Rating_
Feeling or acting as if actually re-living the event, including seeing aspects of the event right before your eyes	_____
Scary dreams related to the event. These dreams can reflect actual or symbolic aspects of the event	_____
Constant and unbidden intense memories of the event such as images, perceptions and thoughts	_____
Experiencing physical distress (i.e., headache, stomach upset, hives, etc.) when faced with thoughts, behaviors or external cues perceived to represent an aspect of the event	_____
Feeling severe emotional distress when confronted with thoughts, behaviors, or external cues perceived to represent an aspect of the event	_____
Difficulty remembering core facts about the event	_____
Lack of motivation or interest in normal activities of daily living	_____
Persistent attempts to avoid people, places and things that may trigger thoughts about the event	_____
No interest in being emotionally close to others	_____
Consistent attempt to avoid anything associated with the event including feelings, thoughts, conversations, etc.	_____

Reaction	_Rating_
No longer expect future personal goals to be realized	_____
Trouble concentrating	_____
Feeling "wound up" or unable to relax	_____
Trouble falling asleep or sleeping normal hours	_____
Feeling "jumpy" or "on edge"	_____

Adapted from Diagnostic and Statistical Manual of Mental Disorders-Fourth Edition *(DSM-IV)*

Chapter 2

Aftermath of Trauma:
Fear and Uncertainty

As New York City entered its twelfth hour in "lockdown" after the terrorist attacks, I finally fell asleep and dreamed.

> *My house is situated between John F. Kennedy and LaGuardia airports and I am sitting alone in my living room. I begin to hear airplanes flying overhead. I run to the window, frantically searching the skies above to determine where the airplanes are heading. I am afraid and think that the airplanes will come crashing through my house, killing me as I look through my living room window. Then, abruptly, there is silence. At first the silence is comforting, but suddenly, the silence turns eerie and begins to crowd me.*

At 5 A.M., I was jolted awake from my dream and during my shower, feeling uneasy, I pondered the dream's implications. I realized that the reality of trauma is both bright and dark: the glare of its starkness forces you to see it in all its devastation while the darkness of its essence robs you of your innocence. September 11th shattered the false sense of security Americans have always held. We faithfully believed ourselves invincible to such catastrophes. I felt uneasy now, because I was forced to view life beyond the insulated world I had occupied just a day ago. I now had to give serious deliberation to the "who, what, at what time and from where" such destructive actions might come. It stretched my mind in uncomfortable directions.

I began mulling over how the silence in my dream turned eerie and how, even in my dream, the silence seemed to resound, taunting me about the practical survival skills I lacked. Yet even then I believed the need to learn those skills was vital if I was to hold any hope of surviving in a world where violent trauma, such as the one I'd suffered, happened. I kept asking myself, *Can I ever again relax in silence as I often had done in the past—to feel the inner peace present in the magical stillness of a moment in time? Will I always be compulsively searching for the potential terror lurking, just as a child who becomes afraid of monsters hiding in the closet in the quiet darkness of the night? And if I submit to such hyper-vigilance, how could I live a normal life?*

With such thoughts whirling uncontrollably in my mind, I stepped out of the shower, toweled off and began to put my clothes on, wondering how I would overcome such a growing fear as it cloaked itself in an unwelcoming, yet undeniable garment of reality. I sighed heavily, considering how I might emotionally anchor myself and what my gut response would be when the sounds of airplanes flying overhead returned.

After dressing, I sat and waited for my escort to an airport now in lockdown. As I waited, my dread of the day ahead multiplied with each passing moment. I arrived at the airport at 7:30 A.M. and shortly after 8 A.M. survivors began filling the waiting room. Despite my fears, I quickly became caught up in a whirlwind of emotions that swept me along as I moved from one survivor to the next.

As I talked to them, the raw emotions of the survivors permeated the office. It was as if I could actually smell the fear, the shock and the bottomless terror gagging my own spirit. The day itself seemed dark and despondent, both quiet and deafening. I could hear the desperation in the voices of these people and see their eyes cloud with fear as they remembered. I was witnessing trauma in its extreme, catastrophic form. The comfort of the commonplace and the joys of everyday lives that we survivors had lived and felt before our joint trauma were slipping away. I was sadly aware that months, even years, might pass before some survivors would truly smile, much less laugh again. So I began my work easing the torment of others at the New York City airport that day, knowing that I was facing the same intense emotional turmoil and distress they were.

By noon, steady streams of anguished people were pouring into the medical office. I met with an United States Customs agent and then a flight attendant who had lost close friends on one of the doomed aircraft. I also spoke individually and in groups of two with at least a dozen of the transit agency's employees. During the more than twelve hours I spent at the airport on that day, mostly listening, I allowed each person the opportunity to begin the process of moving beyond the shock and numbness surrounding the horror of their trauma the day before. I knew that these first meetings could only be the minutest steps on a long and, for many, excruciatingly painful road to healing.

As I saw and talked to more and more survivors, I was asked repeatedly, "Who can know what it was truly like if they have never had the experience of such horror?" Because I too had been there, they felt able to reveal their most painful feelings. Survivors affirmed to me with absolute conviction, "You know, because you were there too. You understand." Rapport seemed to be established almost instantly as they unburdened themselves of their pain. "You calm me. I can talk to you," I was told over and over again as I moved from one survivor to the next.

Trauma Survivor and Helper

Despite all my efforts to ease others' pain, my own resounded within me. By 8 P.M. that evening, now a depository filled with the trauma of others, I was functioning in a semi-automatic state. While my clinical skills were second nature and I knew that these skills were enabling me to connect and empathize with each survivor, I could not ignore my own feelings. I humbly acknowledged that the terror I experienced was as stark as the brightest light in a white room. Previously, the intensity of such terror had been a stranger to me. And I could not help but conclude that the horror of the day before was teaching me a painful lesson—fear and uncertainty were my new instructors.

Ultimately, I knew that I would need help to integrate these lessons into my internal view of the world and to guide others to do the same. *What a complicated situation to be in*, I thought. *How can I continue to be here for others when I also need to come to terms with my own trauma?* There was also a visceral fear inside me: fear of not only working with the raw emotions of so many of the traumatized, but doing so in the wake of a national calamity. So many unknowns were out there and those unknowns were of immense proportion.

I had a professional duty as a clinician on one hand and a need for self-care on the other. Yet my own memories of the event gave me an advantage. I knew that I could help each survivor to understand an important point—that painful and distressing reactions were normal in the aftermath of any trauma. I knew I could share with each survivor the value of talking about his or her feelings, thoughts and reactions as a first step to overcoming and integrating his or her traumatic experiences. I knew that I could teach survivors strategies that would prove helpful in their healing process. All these things I knew and I knew well; the pull to focus exclusively on these abilities was strongly compelling. Yet for all the same reasons, I needed to create the opportunity to do the same things for myself. It was important for me to talk about what I saw, heard, felt and thought. It was necessary to work through my own trauma, the very same trauma I was being called upon to deal with on a professional level.

Common sense told me that for me to be truly helpful to other survivors, my initial need was to take care of myself. Despite personal fears and uncertainty, I began to devise a plan. I anchored this plan into serving both my personal needs and my professional duty. The plan I envisioned would allow me to help others and myself in a parallel fashion.

First, I said to myself, *I need to get support from other mental health professionals*. At the same time, with the help of my mentor, I would have to begin dealing with all the intense emotions attacking me like shards of glass. Constant physical and emotional replenishment was going to be the key to my own healing process and would also help me to stave off professional burnout.

While I was preparing to mobilize resources, I was operating under conditions of chaos, working to create a plan that would help a significantly traumatized community. So, too, the repeated threats of terrorism could elicit further trauma with no defined end point and therefore be even more difficult to contain. I knew I would be working in a chaos that would be ever fluid and fluctuating and that survivors would need different approaches at different stages of their trauma for healing to occur.

Two days later, the crisis-counseling center was relocated from the medical office at the airport to a local hotel. It operated twenty-four hours per day, seven days per week with hotel suites and rooms being used as counseling suites, reception areas and waiting rooms. I was now directing all crisis intervention, grief counseling and other counseling-related activities. I was managing over 150 licensed psychologists, masters-level social workers, nurses and clergy members whose primary task was to try to normalize the expansive range of emotions, thoughts and behaviors expressed by each survivor and family member. The clinician's role was also to share information on how trauma and grief are commonly manifested so survivors could gain a greater understanding of what they were currently feeling and what they might feel over time.

Leading a coalition of mental health clinicians within days after such a cataclysmic set of events was daunting. However, the need to think quickly and creatively during a period of near chaos was therapeutic. It became my central task as I worked vigorously to establish an operation that would deliver the center's clinical services in as efficient, professional and supportive a manner as possible to those suffering so grievously.

This task, admittedly, gave me a sense of control and purpose that had been lacking in the hours after the attack. After escaping the Twin Towers on that terror-filled day, I decided to offer assistance by helping to triage survivors who were obviously in shock. In the midst of chaos, the need to "do something" in order to regain some semblance of control becomes powerful. Like all first responders to disasters, be they medical, mental health, fire, emergency services or police, the trauma assaulting the senses floods back like a tidal wave when immediate tasks are completed and the environment becomes less chaotic and seemingly more manageable. So in tandem with my professional work, I became equally determined to address my own ordeal.

As Steff, a forty-four-year-old father and husband who loves Christian music, remembers his experience and its aftermath, his account provides a personal glimpse into the feelings of those afflicted by the day's events:

At 8:45, a man ran inside. It was one of the technicians who work in my shop. He ran in and said, "The World Trade Center is on fire."

I said, "The Trade Center is on fire?"

He said, "Yeah, the Trade Center is on fire."

We ran around to the corner of the building and as we looked up I saw a red ring of flame around an upper floor of Tower One, the north tower. And the fire was steadily spreading. As a couple of minutes passed, maybe five minutes, I noticed it became two floors with rings of fire around it.

I said, "We're going to lose our main communication system. I do have some equipment in the shop that was slated to go to another facility. We could reprogram that and mount it on top of this building and provide back-up communications should we lose the station on top of the Tower."

So as I was doing that, shortly after 9 A.M., someone came in and said a missile hit Tower Two."

I said, "A missile? So where is the plane that shot this missile?"

"He said, 'We don't know, but we believe that a missile hit Tower Two.'

At that point we were really scrambling. I had almost a dozen great men working, really working hard that day. These technicians were working with me to get antennas and equipment hoisted up to the penthouse on top of the building so we could provide some kind of backup communication.

Around 10 A.M., I turned my back for a few moments.

I said to one of the men, "Okay, make the connection and let's fire this thing up."

In half a minute, maybe forty seconds, I turned back around and it seemed like the building was gone. "No, I can't believe it"' I said. "No, it's just the smoke blocking my view."

Because, you know, the brain can't come to terms with something as catastrophic as that. I looked again. A few moments after that one of the maintenance men from the building staggered across the roof and came up to me.

He said, "The building fell over."

I said, "The building fell over?"

He said, "Yeah! It fell over," meaning to me that this huge structure just fell over and just took out many city blocks and I can only imagine the horror. At that point, I began to faint but I thought, *I have things to do; I can't pass out*. The radio squawked at that point. Communication was up and running.

Well, I remained up on the roof until the second building collapsed. I saw the antenna start to sink and the building start to bend a little bit and the next thing I knew, it just crumbled and disappeared out of my sight. It was just unbelievable what had unfolded in maybe an hour and a half or an hour and forty-five minutes. By that point, what could anyone really say? It just felt like you had to get into battle mode and try to see what you could do to help people. Meanwhile you're having all kinds of thoughts going through your head, like, *Who made it? Who didn't? What's going on?* Phone lines were busy. People were in a panic. People were crying. Just chaos.

As he reflected on the emotions he experienced in the aftermath of September 11th, Steff remembers,

The event itself was painfully sad. It's something that we certainly wouldn't want to go through. We didn't expect that something so horrible could happen and I would never want to go through something like that again, the Lord willing. Well, all I can say is that this period was like an adrenaline rush. Yet I was still in a state of disbelief. After the initial shock, it felt like coming off a high and part of me wanted the high.

Steff's initial response was similar to many emergency first responders in the face of any kind of disaster: complete each task as it arises and function on autopilot, confident that training and experience will take over. With no real reprieves, Steff found himself too tired to think or feel. He returned home after working sixteen to twenty hours, slept a few hours and then would go back to work, starting the cycle again.

As the days turned into weeks, however, he was paying a price. No longer feeling the "high" of purpose and action as tasks were concluded, both physical fatigue and the horror of his experience began to sink in. With time to think, to acknowledge and to feel, memories of his trauma flooded back into his consciousness.

As Steff recalls, his blood pressure soared and the demands of his job, once fueled by adrenaline, became his burden, pulling him down until he buckled under the weight. His mood changed from an almost frenzied state to one of depression: a state of being that survivors soon discover is closely tied to trauma, loss and grief. Steff became increasingly anxious; his sleep was regularly interrupted, his loss of spark apparent.

Steff's distress highlights the potentially deleterious effects of being in perpetual battle mode following a catastrophic event. Such a mode often circumvents the necessary attention survivors need to pay to the emotional and physical effects of trauma in order for recovery and emotional healing to begin. Early on in my attempts to sidestep the same protracted pain and suffering experienced by Steff, I had, like other clinicians, attended several crisis debriefings where we shared our personal reactions. I knew, as survivor and professional, that the temptation to become entangled in the lives of other survivors was well-meaning but professionally unproductive. I was therefore always mindful that I needed to maintain a professional distance in order to discover where I could be most helpful. I also needed to rely on talks with my mentor to deal with potential issues such as that of professional boundaries. I had also begun speaking daily with my mentor as I processed what I was feeling and thinking. As I continued to put in twelve-hour days at the crisis-counseling center, I asked myself the same question each morning: *How can I best manage the dual nature of my life as both first responder and survivor?*

I ultimately decided that in the initial period following the traumatic event, I could best serve the needs of others by using my clinical, supervisory and administrative skills to direct and manage the crisis-counseling services provided by other clinicians who were not direct survivors. I then brought my own trauma to the foreground of my consciousness.

The "What Ifs" and the Struggle with Fear and Uncertainty

In those early weeks, I thought often of September 11th. On that day I had been terrified, plain and simple. The fear and uncertainty stayed with me, casting a surrealistic veil over my actions. During this time, I also found myself reflecting on the "what ifs" of my trauma: What if the stairwell I was traveling down had been impassable? What if I had lingered in my office too long? What if I had been in the elevator when the plane hit? What if I had been on a higher floor? What if I had been in the stairwell when the building collapsed? What if I had died? This last question weighed heavily on my mind as I thought about the impact that my death would have had on my partner, family and friends. I also thought often of the victims I knew and the pain their families were experiencing.

As the days passed, did my fear and uncertainty regularly make themselves known. I was spending twelve hours a day in a hotel near the airport and when airplanes began to fly again I heard their approach and felt the building vibrate. I was so close I even saw people in their seats as an airplane took off and began to ascend directly above me. *What the hell am I doing here?* I asked myself many times over during those weeks as all of us froze momentarily at the sounds and the rumbling of airplanes overhead. To make myself feel better, I jokingly told myself that if my time at the airport did not squelch this new fear of airplanes slamming into buildings, then nothing would. On a professional level, I knew that continued exposure to a fear would, over time, diminish the anxiety attached to it. I would become desensitized. Whether I would have willingly chosen to expose myself so quickly and so intensely is another matter.

Embarking on my own healing journey while serving as a counselor to others experiencing trauma, I had an advantage. Moreover, on a day-to-day basis I was working with others who experienced 9/11. As I observed these survivors and reflected on those I had treated in the past, it was confirmed that the initial trauma reactions I saw spanned the spectrum of emotions and were as numerous and diverse as the unique qualities of each individual. Yet, as a general response, trauma has some unvarying components. Fear and uncertainty are feelings which typically surface very early. The unexpected nature of a traumatic event naturally lends itself to the immediate fear of being caught off-guard with no time to brace against the trauma and no armor to fight against the horror. We all prefer some certainty in our lives. We need to believe we have control over our destiny and that we can maintain that control. So when an event so extraordinary in its devastation occurs, the purpose and the certainty on which we rely vanishes, stripping us of our armor, leaving us feeling vulnerable and naked.

Our fears then throttle into overdrive, for we can no longer predict the next moment of our lives. We become acutely uncertain about the minutes to follow; a bizarrely uncomfortable state of mind results, in which harsh reality and our belief in our ability to control our destinies collide. We do not want to acknowledge that we could lose the battle. This uncertainty about our futures and the fear it engenders quickly moves us to think, feel and behave in ways that are incongruent with whom we were before our traumas.

Although I was working with survivors and families every day and preached the importance of a return to normalcy, approximately two months passed before I decided to venture back into Manhattan. The thought of returning led to emotions that were variations of revulsion and dread. However, on a practical level, I knew that I needed to face my fears in order for emotional healing and recovery to take place. With great trepidation, I made plans to travel throughout a city I felt I no longer knew.

As I stood on the Long Island Railroad train station platform, it felt strange to be looking at the familiar faces of the regular 7:23 A.M. commuters into Pennsylvania Station, New York. The platform felt inconsequentially small, much like the unnerving feeling you may have experienced if you have ever returned to your elementary school and realized how very small it seemed to your adult self.

I listened to the banter among clusters of commuters and wondered how they could engage in such banal pleasantries. I realized that while they had been immersed in their daily routines for the past two months, I had been in the constant company of those who were in terrible pain—a pain so raw as to systematically peel away the very protective layers we wear in our attempts to defend against those events we define as proof positive of life's unfairness.

I suddenly felt worlds apart from my fellow commuters and, I admitted to myself, jealous. These people had the luxury of time to temper the heart-wrenching fear that had pulsed through people directly affected on that terrible day in September. An insidious terror had been seeping into my pores since September 11th and seemed to coagulate with each physical contact between myself and a grieving sister, brother, mother, father, wife, husband, companion, lover or friend. In contrast, my fellow commuters had reached the point where they could easily engage in prosaic banter. *That's as it should be*, I thought, as I made a conscious effort to get into my old rhythm.

The train pulled into the station. As usual people positioned themselves along the platform where they knew the train doors would stop. My movements, however, were creaky, like the brakes of an old bicycle. I found myself being the last to step into the train car. I searched for an empty seat, found one next to a middle-aged man, sat down and immediately began to scan the faces of the car's occupants. *Is anybody here a threat to me?* I thought. *Stop*, I chided myself, knowing that if I continued such thoughts I would push myself into a state of intense anxiety. *Calm down*, I told myself. Taking slow, deep breaths, I reminded myself that my fellow commuters had been riding the train through Manhattan for months since the attacks and had made it back home every evening since then. Forcing myself to focus on similar thoughts, I tried to ease the fear and anxiety that was threatening to derail me.

Three minutes later, the train pulled into the next station and a half-dozen people boarded the car. As they boarded, the air suddenly became weighed down; you could have sliced the tension with a knife. Anyone who has survived a traumatic event richly knows the character of such apprehension. The taste of fear was so terrifying as to be almost incomprehensible. I studied the train's newest passengers. The explanation for such palpable tension became immediately clear: among the passengers was a tall, turban-wearing man of assumed Middle-Eastern descent. He toted a backpack. Looking around, I was amazed at how quickly everyone came right back to a place of alarm and helplessness. This man had unwittingly triggered the same emotions that came to define September 11th. The train car was pin drop silent. The ease of routine commuter conversation completely evaporated.

As the man walked to the back of the car and stood next to the conductor's station facing my section of the train, I saw that people had stopped reading their newspapers, books and magazines. Those who were seated in the opposite direction could no longer see him. Now that he was behind them, their discomfort mounted. They adjusted and re-adjusted themselves in their seats. Several people looked back, ostensibly to stretch themselves. Some stared in the windows in an almost feverish manner, making obvious attempts to catch a glimpse of the Middle Easterner through the reflection. As the station receded in the distance, we all seemed to be holding our breath, suddenly too afraid to exhale. It was unclear what came first—the apprehension pouring out of us or the Middle Eastern man's anxiety. He seemed nervous and fidgety as well. He pulled at his beard, ran his hand quickly several times in succession up and down his face, and with his thumb and index fingers, repeatedly smoothed his eyebrows. *A nervous tic? Are we making him nervous or does he have some other reason to be nervous?* I wondered, watching him repeat the compulsive ritual every few seconds.

The train conductor's arrival in our car seemed to lessen slightly the paralysis and as the minutes passed no new catastrophe happened. It became obvious that even though this barely discernible wisp of tension had dissipated, the resumption of the morning rituals of many aboard the train remained absent—the readers turned not one single page nor did any conversations resume throughout the remainder of the trip. Clearly we were all in a state of controlled panic: except for one woman who, with her head flinging rapidly back and forth, repeatedly looked back at the man. This woman, as she constantly turned around in her seat to see what he might be doing, became our projection, acting out what we all wanted to do. Meanwhile the Middle Eastern man continued his tactile ritual—beard, face and brow, not making eye contact with anyone.

As we entered the tunnel leading into the belly of Pennsylvania Station, people visibly flinched whenever the train car lights flickered, as they often do. In the darkness of the tunnel (in unison, it seemed) we again held our collective breath. Tension made the air enormously suffocating and it seemed almost prudent to hold on to what air we already held. An almost telepathic thought seemed to register simultaneously with us all: *The tunnel would be a dramatic finish to a terrorist act!* As we waited, afraid of the impending doom we seemed convinced was to come at any moment, the lights continued to flicker off and on, mockingly.

Several minutes, feeling like hours, passed. Then we arrived at Pennsylvania Station, unharmed. As commuters moved toward the doors, I watched as a disjointed dance ensued. People gave the man a wide berth. No one seemed to want to be in front of him. As he moved forward, other commuters held back. When he paused in his movement everyone else stopped. Finally the doors opened and he stepped outside. I tried to watch him as he moved into the throngs of people exiting the other cars and then up the stairs, blending in with the thousands of commuters passing through Pennsylvania Station on a weekday morning.

As I followed, I also felt guilty, acknowledging that I had allowed myself to become caught up in a dangerous way of thinking. We all had assumed that we were in the presence of a potential terrorist just because of the way the man looked. I felt embarrassed at how quickly and without empathy we had made this man a target of our fears, stereotypes and projections. I worried that other innocent people like him would be subjected to what he had endured or worse. I wondered at his emotions. *What did he see in our facial expressions, and what did he feel and think about our behavior?*

While nothing catastrophic happened in this incident, in fact, a fundamental change had taken place on September 11th. The attacks caused us all to re-think our worldview about what was now possible. Sadly, we now all seemed easily prone to stereotyping of the sort that was played out on this Manhattan-bound train. Many Arab and Muslim communities in America were probably feeling alienated, stigmatized and discriminated against. *How can we assure our safety in this new world in a way that does not damage us or make us quick to prejudge?* I asked myself. History has shown over and over again, with different groups of people at different times, how dangerous a posture of prejudice can be. Yet I was aware that ethnic hate or distrust can become an easy but unfortunate product of traumatic experience.

In the ensuing months, other survivors of the World Trade Center attacks began to admit to me their new fear of people they assumed to be of Middle Eastern descent. They shared their feelings, tinged with guilt and shame. When they did I told them of my own experience on that Manhattan-bound train. In our discussions, we talked about how fear is a manifestation of feelings of vulnerability, uncertainty and powerlessness, and that the projection of hate and distrust on to something or someone is a vehicle used to gain a false sense of control and predictability. I guided them to the conclusion that if they tackled their fears, distrust would diminish. As trauma survivors, whatever the source, the effect is that our view of the world becomes suddenly skewed, making us vulnerable to the particulars that speak to our trauma.

Along with everything else comes a palpable sense of a future suddenly and irrevocably shortened. Alenna, one survivor, told me she asked herself "What is going to happen next? From where will the next tragedy come? It scares me that I don't have the answers to these questions. The future seems so bleak right now and the best I can do is stay home. I feel more in control. Calmer."

Like Alenna, Brandon reflected on how fear and uncertainty led to incongruities and differences within him. He remembers asking himself:

> Why am I now different? It seems like such a simple question, one that I ask myself over and over again. But it is a question that can only be truly understood by someone who has lived through a horrific incident. Unfortunately, I continued to re-live that day over and over again, pushing away from who I once was.

> In the first few days, I tried to keep a stiff upper-lip. I even believed I was feeling "gung-ho." But I also felt like I needed to burst into tears in order to relieve some of the pressure that was building up inside me.

Other such survivors recall their experiences of fear and uncertainty. In doing so, they show how these emotions manifested themselves and began to disrupt their lives in numerous ways.

Antoinette, an administrator who loves roller-skating, crocheting and reading and is the single mother of two children, ages eleven and twenty-two, remembered as she first recounted to me the chaos of that day,

We moved down the stairs at a snail's pace, it seemed, and I spent the entire time praying, repeating scriptures and silently singing spiritual songs while asking God for guidance.

When I finally reached the mezzanine level, the water was knee deep and I pulled up my skirt to wade through the water. Everything in the lobby area was blown to pieces —the turnstiles, chandeliers and even the revolving doors were off their hinges. As we exited the building, we were commanded to "Keep moving" and "Don't look up." But I looked up and immediately dropped to my knees when I saw that both buildings were in flames.

Minutes later, I caught sight of my cousin, who also worked in the area. We were trying to locate a telephone to let our families know that we were together and both okay, when a deafening noise erupted. It sounded like a warplane was descending as a great cloud of smoke appeared. Although we started running for our lives, the cloud of smoke followed us and eventually engulfed us.

We found ourselves in the basement of a nearby Spanish restaurant, where, because of the impact from the building collapse, raw meat and food lay all over the floor. There were civilians, police and military personnel walking through the carnage. We retrieved water from the restaurant's refrigerators to wash away some of the dust. Out of nowhere, I suddenly became extremely nervous about being in the restaurant. I told my cousin to take off her high heel shoes, grab two bottles of water and a handful of paper towels. We left the restaurant and headed toward the Brooklyn Bridge. When we got there, we encountered hundreds of people walking across it. As we crossed the bridge, the second tower collapsed and we all fell to the pavement.

And, as she later recalled, remembering the aftermath of her trauma on that day,

I stayed in bed and was afraid to leave my house. Then I felt anxiety and uncertainty about my future. The anxiety stayed with me for a long, long time.

I also felt tremendous sadness for the people lost. It was incomprehensible to me to know that I could lose such dear friends in a twinkling of an eye. I had many sleepless nights.

Alyce, a forty-three-year-old administrative secretary who loves traveling, is an active Episcopalian and the single mother of a twenty-three-year-old college student remembers:

On that morning, I walked leisurely down the hill to the subway station. As the train approached downtown Manhattan, near Christopher Street, it started to delay. As we crept along from station to station I could hear emergency vehicle sirens from outside, penetrating the tunnels of the subway stations. I remember saying to a woman across from me, "Whatever is going on out there, it's serious."

As we finally approached Chambers Street, there was an announcement over the PA system telling us that there was a smoke condition and that the train would terminate at Chambers Street. As I exited to the street, I placed my hand in my handbag searching for my cell phone to call a coworker to let her know that I would be a little late. I noticed that people were looking up and pointing. I, in turn, did the same and almost lost my bearings.

The hole in the building seemed to be in the general location of the offices where I worked and I began counting the floors trying to figure out just where this horrible tragedy occurred. Suddenly, hoards of people started running toward me. I turned and ran about three blocks and ended up at a nearly completed construction site with about six other individuals. We were crying and praying as mass hysteria let loose all around us. I eventually braved the outdoors and headed north. I again pulled my cell phone from my pocketbook and dialed my daughter's number, dialing and redialing until I reached her. Crying, I told her that I was all right and that I was heading north and would call her back. Ten minutes

later, I ran into a childhood friend and we agreed to venture out into the chaos together. We boarded the A train and it slowly took us to 42nd Street, but at that station the train went out of service and discharged all passengers. My friend and I walked west in search of a bus, seeing many along the way, but none stopped because they were full beyond capacity. We kept walking.

After walking approximately one hundred blocks, we reached Riverside Drive and 159th Street. With my feet blistered, we walked across the nearest bridge into the Bronx, New York. Once in the Bronx, I called two close friends of mine. They told me to stay put and arrived in a car several minutes later to take me home. We cried and cried together.

For Alyce, as she later recalled, "While it was all happening and in those first few days I never once thought that my life would change forever. This was the beginning of my denial. As the days passed, I pretty much found myself in the fetal position, physically and mentally exhausted."

Essentially, for trauma survivors in the early stages of healing, fear and uncertainty seem to be the main constants. And as later revealed by Antoinette and Alyce, the effects of fear and uncertainty crept into many aspects of their life. Also plaguing survivors is the fear that something very important was lost—a way of life. Their thoughts race to the question of how they will ever get back to where they were before. "Will I ever be the same?" is a question often asked. "Will I be whole again?" Many then become entwined in a seemingly never-ending emotional bind: a poisoned necklace of helplessness, fear and uncertainty.

As for me, for weeks I saw flashes of my trauma: bodies falling from above my office window, planes hitting the building, the flaming hole that the plane left in its wake. My mind also created other potential horrors that suddenly seemed possible: buildings I passed through could suddenly blow up; I would see planes in the sky and envision another plane attack on a building, a bomb going off on a train that I boarded. These images were indeed distressing, creating tension throughout my body. But I did not fight them. I allowed

these images to run their course, because I knew I had to imagine the worst in order to move beyond my ordeal. My healing process began much like the mechanism that drives a pendulum; the dynamic of my process was such that it had to swing to its extreme emotional point in order to gain the necessary momentum to settle back to the plumb line of the ordinary. If you are a trauma survivor, you most likely could experience similar fears, recreating your own experiences. Do not bury them. Work through them.

Reliving Trauma through the Senses

Through the years I have also observed that many other survivors relive their traumas through flashbacks and nightmares about losing control and feeling helpless. For many, sleep offers no relief and flashbacks, of course, come unbidden. And while survivors relived their trauma through their anxiety, uncertainty and fear, many also felt their trauma through every sensory organ. Some spoke of their bodies as refusing to be still. They paced their homes, unable to sit for more than a few minutes at a time, and scanned and re-scanned their environment for any hint of danger. The sights and sounds of city life outside their window became an enemy—a trigger. Dust, the shrieking of train brakes, trucks traveling on a bumpy street, the sound of water running, sunshine like that on 9/11, all coalesced into a fear so enormous as to challenge everything the survivor believed in that split second before trauma struck. For some, panic attacks became constant and their bodies took them on emotional roller coaster rides, while many had the affliction of unrelenting anxiety.

Trauma and the Body's Response

Listening to trauma survivors and reflecting to my own journey has taught me that trauma not only assaults the mind but can also wreak havoc on the body, leading the person who has experienced the trauma to feel physically exhausted. When we experience trauma, our bodies and the biochemical processes in our bodies often become topsy-turvy for a while.

Encoded in our autonomic nervous system is the "fight or flight" response, a survival mechanism whereby neuro-transmitters such as epinephrine, norepinephrine, dopamine, serotonin and others

are pumped throughout our bodies when needed. If we interpret an event as life-threatening, this pure survival instinct shuts down functions that are no longer needed and focuses energy on those functions necessary to keep us alive. In addition to physiological changes such as increased respiration and accelerated heart rate, mental activity also speeds up, so that, in the midst of traumatic experiences, many survivors speak of the events they've experienced as if they unfolded in slow motion.

Be comforted that this survival response serves us very well when danger is imminent. If not for the "fight or flight" response, we surely would have perished as a species long ago. However, the biochemicals associated with this response to danger may become our enemy when the immediate threat is gone. If you find, as many survivors do, that this frightening response goes on after danger fades or returns again and again. When sustained for too long a period, this survival instinct wears down the body and potentially leaves us with little strength to react to real-life dangers when we may actually need that energy.

Instead, we become jumpy, agitated and in a constant state of readiness, ambivalent about our choice of action. Our response to trauma accelerates to overload, manifesting itself in pure panic and uncontrollable terror at those things that once were the mundane backdrops of our daily surroundings. Fight or flee, but from what? We search for the danger that our bodies tell us is right before our eyes, yet we cannot see it. Our vigilance increases even further as we frantically scan our environment for the elusive peril. Our thoughts join in as our mind tries to make sense of our physical and emotional reactions, the three eventually forging an alliance. Now aligned, our minds, emotions and bodies inevitably find something to stand in for the danger we cannot see, hear, smell or touch. That "something" could be a previously benign ray of sunlight through a window blind that comes to represent one of a growing number of triggers to reliving our traumatic experience.

When this response mounts a constant assault on a survivor, avoidance becomes more and more attractive. I have heard from survivors many variations of how anxiety, fear and uncertainty changed their lives. To stay put and be still provides a false sense of certainty and control. Therefore, simply stepping outside the comfort of home may become the most frightening act; fear may become so intense that life seems as if it must be put on hold indefinitely. The person's life becomes smaller in order to avoid the fear of the unknown. As I have seen, such avoidance eliminates the opportunity to remember and thus come to terms with your fear and diminishes the opportunity to heal.

Conquering Fear and Uncertainty

After my own traumatic experience, I began to think about what it takes to overcome the fear, uncertainty and anticipatory dread. How can those who have suffered a violent encounter ultimately stare down the harrowing images of death and destruction and emerge victorious against the once unthinkable? Reflecting on other trauma survivors I have known and treated, I have come to feel and believe that within us all there is the capacity to heal from devastating experiences and that the human spirit can be tenacious and resilient.

Chapter 2 Resilience Tips

- When reexperiencing the trauma thorough flashbacks, nightmares and anxiety, remind yourself that these experiences are normal and that they will fade over time.

- Following a nightmare, try to mentally rewrite the nightmare in your mind (i.e., add a safe person to the dream; change the ending) and keep the new "script" in mind just as you go to sleep at night.

- Do not get mentally caught up in what you cannot control.

- Do not bury your feelings. Allow yourself to fully remember so that your mind can digest and resolve the event.

- Remember that the ongoing experience of anxiety and fear taxes the body, mind and spirit as well as creating a less optimal space for effective action. Exercise, eat a balanced diet and engage in relaxing activities to help you manage the physical and mental consequences of traumatic shock and its aftereffects.

EXERCISE

Following a life-altering event, feelings of apprehension and dread may occur. Fear and anxiety may be specific to the traumatic event or may feel more generalized. To help reduce persistent fear or anxiety, try some of the following exercises:

DEEP BREATHING:

Breathing to reduce overall tension: Get in a comfortable position. Close your eyes. Mentally scan your body for areas of tension. Inhale deeply and slowly through your nose and into your abdomen. Exhale through your mouth and count "one." Focus on the feel of your breath and continue counting your exhalations. Continue for five to ten minutes in sets of five exhalations.

Breathing focused on the shoulders, neck and face: Use the above deep breathing exercise for one to two minutes. Then pull your shoulders up your ears to tense the muscles in your shoulders and neck. Hold that position for a count of five, then let your shoulders drop. Notice the difference between tension and relaxation in your shoulders. Repeat at least three times. Next, squeeze your eyes closed as tightly as you can. Feel the tension in your face. Hold the tension for a count of five. Then, still keeping your eyes shut, relax your face. Repeat at least three times.

Relaxing the whole body: Get in a comfortable position. Take a deep breath. Slowly breathe out and silently say "calm." Continue deep breathing saying "calm" during exhalation. Slowly let go of the tension in your body, focusing on any area that is tight during your exhalation. Continue deep breathing as you tell your body to relax even more.

DISTRACTION TECHNIQUES:

Touching: Take an object in your hand and feel its weight. Study the material of which it is made. Focus on the feel of the contours in your hand. Fully concentrate on getting to know every aspect of the object. Continue until you feel relaxed.

Colors: Look around you. Silently identify the colors you see. Continue until you feel relaxed.

IMAGERY:

Imagery entails forming mental impressions that include all your senses: hearing, sight, touch, smell and taste. For example, imagine a beach. Add the smell of the ocean, the sounds of the waves, the taste of salt in the air, the feel of sand passing through your fingers. Select images that work best for you. Below are two suggestions to get you started.

Warm light: Practice deep breathing for one to two minutes. As you continue to relax your body imagine a warm, soothing light coming through the floor and into the soles of your feet. Allow the light to reach your ankles and continue up your leg. Imagine the light relaxing your thighs and hips. Allow the warm light to move through your stomach and then your chest. Let the light travel to your fingers and arms. Imagine the light calming the muscles in your neck. Breath deeply and slowly as you allow the light to soothe your entire body. When ready, slowly open your eyes and stretch.

Scenery: Pick a favorite setting. It could be a forest, a beach or a vacation spot. Visualize yourself there, remembering to engage all your senses as you imagine the setting. Make it peaceful, safe and comfortable.

Try to practice imagery at least twice per day.

Note: Selected breathing technique features were adapted from The Relaxation and Stress Reduction Workbook *(Fifth Edition) by M. Davis, E. Eshelman and M. McKay (2000) MJF Books: NY*

Chapter 3

Trauma and Grief

In the days that follow trauma, as shock and numbness wear off, loss can no longer be denied, just as life cannot be rewound like a tape to replay or reorder or in some way change the sequence of events that define our trauma. To sustain a sudden loss is a condition that leads many to feel abandoned and helpless. The aching propels the survivor to a loathsome place.

Grief is that place. After my own trauma on September 11th, I grieved for the people I knew who had perished. I grieved for the security guards I greeted each morning as I boarded the elevator to reach my office. I grieved the loss of the sense of safety I had known and the innocence that security implied. I grieved the loss of the daily routine I had come to expect. I also felt tremendous grief and sorrow for the thousands of people who became victims that day and the hundreds of thousands directly affected by their deaths—the children, spouses, parents, brothers, sisters, grandparents, uncles, aunts and friends. My grief was a place filled with pain and longing, the pain of grief attached to my losses and the longing for the life before my trauma. Over the years, those I treated have often told me of their needs to speak candidly to someone of the multitude of emotions they felt. I now felt that need personally. I spoke many times to my mentor about the emotional heaviness inside me.

Being able to convey what you are feeling to a friend, counselor, another survivor, family member or sometimes several of these individuals can be of great solace and is a healing step. Don't bury your feelings. Even though it may be difficult, especially at first, talk to someone you trust about the heaviness in your own heart. It will lighten the burden you, as a survivor, carry.

Grief Patterns

Many to whom I have spoken say that grief feels like a transformation of their trauma, revealed in another painful dimension. After a while, many survivors say, they discovered that trauma and grief were processes that ebb and flow together in unpredictable ways, constantly throwing their minds, emotions and bodies off balance. Like trauma itself and each survivor's unique response to it, grief does not willingly submit to logical reasoning. In the days to weeks following life-altering events, many find themselves in processes that are the antithesis of rationality.

Grief emerges in many ways and at different times, with varying levels of intensity. Some tell of experiencing a number of permutations of grief at different periods and sometimes several distinctive waves in a single minute, hour or day. Many speak of feeling empty inside, depressed or angry. Some reveal that their minds torment them with flashes of that which was lost, the way things used to be—a scent, a picture or a song. And others say their hearts feel punctured and seem to cry out with wishful longing.

Some struggle mightily to pull themselves out of such deep despair. As Antoinette shares, "My grief was mostly pure sadness about the people I lost. I cried, yelled and screamed in pain. My body was jumpy. I smoked a lot of cigarettes and began drinking more than I ever had in my life." The feeling Antoinette reveals reminded me that when we are confronted with grief, we frantically search for ways to cope and assuage.

Large numbers of survivors try to numb the pain of their grief as a way of coping with what some describe as sorrow so searing that it seems to rip holes in the very fabric of their souls, leading them to feel more like victims than survivors. Still others, like Antoinette, admit to having taken up smoking or smoking more if they previously used tobacco. Others talk of drinking more than ever or using mood-altering drugs.

These negative means of coping obviously complicate the grieving process. They numb the emotions but leave the pain. Survivors who utilize these must realize eventually that they need to pull themselves away from further complicating their lives through overdependence on drugs or alcohol. Children, spouses and other loved ones can help bring the grief-stricken through the pain. Many survivors tell me that such loved ones pulled them away from the brink of alcoholism and other forms of self-medication.

Mara, a thirty-five-year-old accounting specialist and single mother of a ten-year-old-daughter, found it extremely difficult to acknowledge and accept that she was grieving a great loss. For Mara, the terror began on her way to work on September 11th,

I entered the subway and was pleasantly surprised that the downtown E train platform wasn't crowded and the train was almost empty. We seemed to be traveling at the speed of light and before very long we pulled into the World Trade Center station. I exited the train and began to walk through the concourse level as I had done every weekday for the past eleven years. I passed the usual shops and restaurants. I had just passed a clothing store when a woman began screaming that there was a bomb in the building. I froze immediately, but wondered if I should take her seriously. I decided to continue on my way, because people around me were going about their business, talking, walking into shops and heading toward the building elevators.

As I continued on, suddenly people began running toward me. I turned and began running as well. I was terrified, because I didn't know where the bomb was and therefore I felt like I was running through a minefield. I wanted desperately to get out of the building, yet my heart was pounding so fast that I could hardly run. I panicked. I began crying, because I'm claustrophobic and I felt that I couldn't breathe. Some stranger kept telling me that it would be all right, but I ignored that person, mumbling, "I need to get out. I need to get out."

Outside, I was confronted with a gaping black hole with

flames in One World Trade Center. I immediately called my fiancé from a nearby payphone. When he answered, I began yelling, crying and screaming and at the same time, asking him whether he knew what happened. Meanwhile, he was yelling for me to get out of the building, screaming that the television reporters said that a plane crashed into my building. I, in turn, was yelling at the top of my lungs that I was already outside the building. Eventually, we stopped yelling over each other and were able to hear what the other was saying. I poured all kinds of change into the pay phone, because I did not want to hang up with him. I was too terrified to hang up.

All of a sudden he said, "Oh, shit!"

And at that very moment, I looked up and witnessed the attack on the second building. My fiancé was yelling again for me to get the hell out of there because a second plane just hit tower two.

I couldn't believe what I was seeing. The telephone slipped from my hand and my jaw dropped open. I saw bodies "flying" out of the building. I saw people on fire jumping. People on the ground went running for cover. A man saw me standing there, paralyzed, and told me to run north. "North" had no meaning to me. I just knew to run away from the building. There were literally thousands of people on the streets, elbow to elbow. There were police and sirens everywhere. It just seemed like one big noise.

I became afraid to move. I thought about all of the landmark buildings in the area. "Is there another plane? What will be crashed through next?" I thought of my ten-year-old daughter and started to cry. At that moment, I believed in my heart that I would not make it home. Ever. I believed that I was going to be killed. I began to pray feverishly.

Then I saw a mentally handicapped person who worked in my company's mailroom. He asked if I could help him get home, because he only knew one way to get to and from home and work. I assured him that I would get him home safely. At that moment, I felt like he was an angel sent to me from heaven, because I no longer had time to be afraid. I had to focus on getting him home to his family. We walked for about three minutes before we felt and heard an awful rumbling and a roaring sound. The ear-splitting noise coupled with that of the rumbling shook me to no end. I looked up and then down, because I expected either the sky above or the ground beneath me to open up and suck me in.

It took almost two hours before we reached my grandmother's house. My friend called his family to let them know that we arrived there safely. My grandmother got us something to eat and we watched the news in stunned silence. We left her house around 5:30 P.M. I was afraid to take the subway, but my friend needed to get home.

In Mara's case, trauma haunted every waking hour after the attack and grief slowly began to define her. She felt severely depressed and had no interest in herself. She felt distant from her child. She stopped cleaning her home or cooking. She spent most of her day in bed. She experienced flashbacks—visual, olfactory, tactile and auditory. She saw what she had gone through unfolding in her mind's eye over and over. She heard it in every sound coming from within her home and outside her front door. She breathed in the smells of that day. A touch from another or the feel of an object could send her reeling back in time. For an excruciating period, she gave up and surrendered to despair. She shut herself off from everyone and everything and stayed locked inside herself. As Mara explained:

It was like I died inside. I stopped living. I isolated myself from my family and friends. I would cry for hours until I threw up. All kinds of other thoughts would go through my head, thoughts like "I have to be prepared." I was paralyzed with fear.

I began to look at the calendar very differently. Any holiday was a potential day for terror. And the time of the event was also a marker for me. I would not allow myself to be on the subway at that time of day. I basically lived in a constant fear of the unknown. I was no longer able to think or act for myself. I waited for people to tell me what to do, to instruct me. When I was told to show up for an appointment, I showed up, but that was all. I couldn't live or make decisions for myself.

I believed that the world was out of control and that it was coming to a violent end. At one point, I decided I didn't want to be in the world anymore. There was no longer anything to believe in except my daughter.

Displaying Grief

As with Mara, I have witnessed many survivors get to know grief much more intimately. It has become evident that there are as many ways to grieve as there are survivors of trauma. Some hold in their grief and refuse to talk about the events they've suffered even with close relatives and friends. Some report feeling that they must be "strong" for others. Or perhaps they hope that time will soften the heartache. Others allow their pain to leak out only in small doses lest they become overwhelmed by their emotions. Still others wear their grief on their sleeves, acutely feeling every sorrowful nuance and riding grief's every wave of despair. For many, grief and loss are perceived as paths, winding around in circles of unwanted painful remembrances.

Jennifer, who lost her husband in a car accident, talked of persistent anxiety attacks, excessive sleeping and regular nightmares. She felt numb, melancholy and lethargic. She also admitted to being gripped firmly in the clutches of survivor's guilt, believing the question "why not me?" to be valid and worthy of great consideration and contemplation. She often sat up in the early hours of the day wracked with guilt because it was not she who had died.

I had the distinct impression that she related to many people and typically moved in a world where they were securely at her side. On the day of her husband's death, she told me that she had seen and interacted with friends and acquaintances before, during and immediately following the event. She knew many and she knew them well, enjoying relationships that were decades old. Yet afterward, for a period of time, she stayed home alone, sleeping up to eighteen hours a day, and not calling friends or loved ones. A "doer," she stopped being active and lost herself in the grip of a grief so palpable that she no longer sought relief. She cut off the very thing that helped to define her—her family and friends.

She informed me that she had lost her appetite and suffered from persistent diarrhea and blinding headaches. She also said that she had never "truly mourned" her husband's death. As I've said, grief and loss can manifest in innumerable ways. Perhaps never truly mourning translates into an inability to accept that one is grieving, a state of being that is, admittedly, very difficult. For many, the deep sadness is so beyond their normal scope of reality that they try to reject it. Yet they feel its intensity nonetheless. Intense grief and loss may cause sufferers to not only reject its reality, but in the process to reject a great deal of that which defined their worlds and their places in them.

Working with Jennifer and other survivors, we have discussed the importance of not only facing their grief but of accepting the process of grief. I try to hold out hope against despair. Though I know it is difficult, I have tried to be like a persistent white spot in the field of the darkness felt by such survivors—urging, demanding and encouraging them to step into the light.

What is Grief Anyway?

Some survivors admit that they do not know what grief is all about, while others believe that grief follows some formula strictly calibrated to time. Roger, a man whose loved one met a violent death, ticked off the stages of grief to me, one by one, as if reciting from a tattered and well-read family list passed down from generation to generation: "First you are in shock for a few hours and then you cry off and on for a couple of days. You cry again at the wake and funeral, and after a few weeks you pretty much forget about it, you know, move on."

While this idea of grief is very controlled indeed, the reports of others with whom I've talked about their grief vary only in the specifics, not the process. Most fully believe that after a certain amount of time (usually a maximum of three to four months), freedom from any emotional signs of grief should be realized. Therefore, when this does not occur for the majority of trauma survivors, feelings of guilt and inadequacy creep into and further complicate their grieving process.

The Tangibles and Intangibles of Grief

Listening to many tell about the variations of grief, I often discuss how traumatic experiences are not merely synonymous with "having a bad day, week, or month." Every traumatic event seems to lead to a loss of "things," both tangible and intangible. There is the tangible loss of a person or perhaps the physical loss of a limb or object. But also experienced are intangible losses such as the loss of an ideal, the way things used to be—a treasured way of life. It is these combined losses that contribute to the intensity of suffering, in both unique and common ways.

I try to guide each survivor through the use of dialogue, which revolves around the fact that intangible and tangible losses following trauma can often be devastating. Therefore, there is the task of learning not only how each person uniquely experiences these losses without calibration to time, but also how each may best begin to heal and recover from their losses in the aftermath.

Some survivors, I have found, were reluctant to seek any help, priding themselves on their past abilities to successfully manage difficulties in their lives. Some talked of raising children, others of successfully juggling careers and maintaining other outside interests. These survivors often could not grasp the concept of receiving guidance outside of themselves, even as their families and friends grew increasingly concerned as they were systematically shut out of the survivor's lives.

In working with people who feel this way, I attempt to reinforce their knowledge of themselves and their assets, acknowledging and praising their many accomplishments and to empathize with their wish to reclaim the people they were before their trauma. I also ask them about the strategies they used to handle other traumatic events they encountered before. "Something like this has never happened to me before," the person usually responds.

"Well," I ask, "in the past when you did not know about something, how did you go about finding out about it?"

"I would research the subject, ask friends about it, or even take a course on it," many reply.

I tell them, "In order to understand how best to handle a new set of experiences and events, you have to first gain knowledge about it. In the case of traumatic events, you have to determine how to deal with the normal responses that follow, because they are distressing and painful. There are tools you can learn that will help you deal with your pain."

"Does this make sense to you?" I ask.

"Yes it does," they typically reply.

An exercise that has proved quite effective among the survivors I have worked with is to make a list of your past strengths and assets that helped in previous difficult circumstances. Refer to this list when you feel depleted and hopeless.

Multiple Traumas

Over the years, as I've worked with more and more survivors, I have learned that some have survived multiple traumas such as the deaths of loved ones or have witnessed violence, such as the murder of a loved one or have survived violence, rape or incest in addition to the trauma for which they consulted me. Unfortunately, in a number of these cases, the survivors had never worked through the previous traumas and the new trauma triggered emotions tied to previous ones. For some of these people, grief seemed to permeate their being. Everything around them seemed to be colored by a cloak of sorrow. For them, grief became a part of their very being.

One of my clients, Liz, recalled that her grief felt acutely familiar. She had felt the same emotions when her mother died. She remembered that she withdrew from her family back then, slipping away and crying alone. *I could not let them see me weak, falling apart*, she remembered thinking. *I have to be the strong one, in control.*

As I spoke with Liz, she began to bring her prior ordeal to a level of awareness previously inaccessible to her. She came to realize that if she suppressed her recent trauma as she had her mother's death, she would hinder her healing from both. She then began the process of working through both traumas simultaneously as to her, they "felt much the same."

In therapy I have found that survivors must begin to address and come to grips with prior traumas in order to cope with a present one. For instance, one traumatic experience that often seems to defy elucidation in its victims is childhood sexual abuse. Many survivors of child sexual abuse speak of how the abuse annihilated their youthful innocence and severely damaged their beliefs in the inherent goodness of others.

As Carol, a thirty-five-year-old mother whose child died recently, recalled:

My mother was in some kind of cult when I was eight. I don't really remember much before then. We were living with tons of people, a lot of adults. There were other kids there, too, older kids. I don't remember going to school back then. All I remember was doing a lot of chores and trying to stay out of the way of the men. I didn't like the way they stared at me. My mother didn't seem to notice.

I remember when the other kids started staying up with the adults and for a while, I was told to go to bed early. Then, one day, my mother took me by the hand and brought me to one of those men's rooms. I tried to tell her I didn't want to go, that I didn't like the men there. But she wouldn't listen. In fact, she kept telling me to shut up. I tried to get away from her, but she just held my wrist tighter and tighter. It hurt.

She literally threw me into the room and shut the door, leaving me with a big, ugly man. He raped me. When he fell asleep, I ran out of the room and then out of the house. I remember running for what seemed like miles across this big open field. I hid until I heard people. I thought they were looking for me so I ran some more.

They eventually found me and brought me back to the house. I was in a daze for weeks. I felt numb. I wouldn't talk to anyone, not even my mother. I hardly ate and when I did, I threw up. I was scared all the time because I thought it could happen again at any second. I tried to stay out of the house as much as possible and at night my body shook until I fell asleep.

In reflecting on that trauma, Carol explained her feelings, finally putting words to a long-dormant pain.

My mother abandoned me. She didn't protect me. She became my enemy, someone who participated in hurting me.

This realization felt so painful. It pierced my heart and I thought it would bleed away into nothingness. I guess this was my grief, a pierced heart caused by a mother who abandoned me.

For Carol, her present grief at losing her child to cancer revolved around not only the trauma of this experience but also grief from the past, when she had lost belief in her caretaker and assumed protector. She spoke as if she no longer expected anything positive in her life. Because of her trauma, by this time internalized, she merely existed, not living life to its fullest. Carol's sense of self-worth unraveled in the face of her new trauma, leading her to seek help. We began to integrate her past and present experiences by talking about the "elephant in the middle of the room" that no one had talked about with her before—her feelings of being damaged and unwanted. Only through the acknowledgment of what she had once lost could Carol begin to heal from her new trauma.

Joyce, a lover of reading and crocheting and a forty-six year-old food service worker had endured two attacks on the World Trade Center. As she talked of her new trauma, she said:

On that morning, I woke up at 5:30 A.M. and prepared for work. I turned on the television and the weatherman promised a lovely day. That day was also my friend's birthday and I planned to take him out after work to celebrate. I left the house feeling really happy.

By 8:30 A.M., I had already been working an hour and was close to finishing the catering portion of my workday. Then, something hit the building. I was knocked to my knees.

"They came back to kill us," I said to one of my supervisors, immediately flashing back to the 1993 bombing.

We all rushed to the window. When we looked out we saw a body lying on top of a nearby roof and a security guard walking along the edge of the same roof. We all turned to run out of the room, but when we reached the door there was so much smoke we were forced to turn back toward the kitchen area.

I called my mother and told her, "They're back to kill us again and I don't know if I will make it out this time." I remember thinking that if I died at least I would finally be with my two children, one killed in 1976 and the other in 1996.

The smoke seemed to clear somewhat so we all decided to head for the staircase. By the time we reached the lobby, it was dark and wet and bricks lay about everywhere.

Outside, we began walking away from the building when someone yelled, "Run!" The building was coming down.

The ground shook and a big cloud that looked like the Devil himself seemed to come right at me and it got very, very dark, shutting out my vision. I fell to the ground and two men covered my body with their own and told me not to move. When the air cleared enough for us to see again, we got up and headed toward a nearby bank. I told them that I didn't want to go into any more buildings. I walked away.

Joyce's previous ordeals at different periods in her life, especially the loss of her only two sons complicated her suffering of this new trauma. The deaths of her children, both lost in early adulthood, haunted her. She related having little social and family support during these devastating events and therefore carried her grief alone. "I have become a closet crier," she noted. Yet tears still welled in her eyes as she spoke of how she had lost the two most precious beings in her life. So, in many ways, to acknowledge the enormity of her recent ordeal was to add another heavy burden to her heart.

Even after so many years of grief, she seemed to have a sense of resignation during the course of her last escape from death. She gave the impression that she felt a sense of relief when death seemed probable, as if twenty-four years of grieving the death of her children was a burden she could only lay down through her own death. The little joy she felt from her work and the friendships that she developed with her coworkers crumbled after her latest trauma. The place where she had been traumatized, now gone, had symbolized for her "something that gave me satisfaction," if only sporadically.

If, like Joyce and Carol, you are the survivor of multiple traumas and are in the midst of a sometimes excruciatingly painful
process, it is good to receive guidance in coping with your past as well
as your recent suffering. Let me share with you the fact that working
through the grief and loss caused by these experiences can enable you
to rediscover a full life. This is a difficult task indeed, but know that
there can be a rewarding life for you again. For many of the survivors
I have worked with, hope for the future eventually came along with
the realization that there were people who cared unconditionally
about how they felt, what they thought and who were willing to share
the burden and guide them along the path to healing. I believe you
too can find such support if you reach out.

Chapter 3 Resilience Tips

- Grief is a normal reaction when one suffers a traumatic loss and often occurs in stages: denial, anger, bargaining, depression, acknowledgment and finally, acceptance. In the case of more than one tragedy you must go through the processing of each of these losses.
- If you have suffered other past traumas let them come to the surface. Write down what you are feeling.
- Do not turn to alcohol and mood-altering drugs. They only complicate the healing process. Get professional help if you have become a substance abuser.
- Reach out to others and talk not only of your pain and loss in the present but also of your losses in the past. This will ultimately help you to move through the total process of grief even if you were unable to do so at the time of the first trauma.
- Be realistic about the time it will take to feel better, especially if you have multiple losses. In other words, allow grief to run its course and do not set an unrealistic timeline of recovery.
- Be extra gentle with yourself, especially if you have experienced multiple losses. Consider seeking professional help so you can find support in the difficult task of integrating past and present traumas.

EXERCISE

Grief is generally an intense emotional state associated with loss that each individual experiences in his or her own unique way. Below are some of the more common feelings, thoughts, physical reactions and behaviors people experience during the grief process. Read each item in all the categories. Using the rating scale below, rate the intensity of each item that applies to you. Add any other feelings, thoughts, behaviors, or physical reactions that may not be listed and rate those using the same scale.

> 1= Almost Never   3= Most of the Time
> 2= Occasionally   4= Always

FEELINGS	RATING
Sad	_____
Depressed	_____
Angry	_____
Irritable	_____
Sense of hopelessness	_____
Helpless	_____
Guilt	_____
Other: _____	_____
Other: _____	_____
TOTAL SCORE	_____

THOUGHTS	RATING
How could this happen?	_____
My life is ruined.	_____
The situation is hopeless.	_____
The event is entirely my fault.	_____
Other: _____	_____
Other: _____	_____
TOTAL SCORE	_____

BEHAVIORS	RATING

Tearfulness, crying   _____
Throwing objects   _____
Yelling, screaming   _____
Withdrawal from others   _____
Other: _____   _____
Other: _____   _____
TOTAL SCORE   _____

PHYSICAL*   **RATING**
Headaches   _____
Upset stomach   _____
Nausea, vomiting   _____
Muscle soreness   _____
Body trembles   _____
Other: _____   _____
Other: _____   _____
TOTAL SCORE   _____

Strongly consider a physical examination to rule out any medical conditions

CATEGORY: **FEELINGS**

If your total score is greater than 18, try one or two of the following exercises.

    Allow yourself to experience an emotion but try not to let it go
    let the emotion spiral out of your control.
    Think of times when you felt differently.
    Write down how you feel in a journal.
    Seek professional help, if necessary.

CATEGORY: **THOUGHTS**

If your total score is greater than 12, Try one or two of the following exercises:

    Practice positive self-statements.
    Repeat affirmations.
    Focus on positive events in your life.
    Practice thought-stopping.

CATEGORY: **BEHAVIORS**

If your total score is greater than 12, Try one or two of the following exercises.

    Engage in an activity that makes you feel competent.
    Do something positive in the moment.
    Talk to someone whom you feel will be supportive.
    Practice deep breathing exercises.

CATEGORY: **PHYSICAL**

If your total score is greater than 14, Try one or two of the following exercises.

    Get active.
    Do exercises.
    Eat healthy, balanced meals.
    See a physician if necessary.
    Take medication as prescribed.
    Get enough sleep.

Chapter 4

Trauma and Denial

"Why do you have that picture on the wall?" Harry, a survivor, asked.

The picture to which he referred is of the World Trade Center Towers, decimated during the tragic events of September 11th. I hung the picture almost four months to the day after the event. I believe it took me that amount of time to come to terms with the chain of events of that day, of which, for me, the picture is a symbolic icon. Coming to terms with my trauma was an ongoing process that was occurring both consciously and unconsciously. I talked about the event, re-lived it through words and images and examined its impact on my life. Yet in the end, the unconscious act of symbolically acknowledging my trauma may best be viewed in the simple act of my being able to hang that picture.

However, be aware that like me and like many survivors I've counseled, you can reach the point where you acknowledge the trauma you've suffered and begin to move on. As with everything in life, trauma does not occur in a vacuum. Each survivor brings with them to his or her recovery process past experiences personality traits and prior ways of coping with adversity. Then trauma, with its many subtle facets, coalesces according to the disposition of the individual, so much so that one person's interpretation and response to the same ordeal may be entirely different from another's.

Acknowledging Trauma

For a number of survivors, denial is a potent defense against the previously unthinkable. It offers them the possibility of fantasy: the ability to rewrite the horror visited upon them in the most benign form—the fantasy of normality. It is a fantasy that is very obvious in its seduction, seeming to offer relief from the unfathomable. And denial can have such nuance that one can maintain it even in the face of clear distress. Yet, while seemingly benign, I saw that for some survivors denial was also dangerous in that it undermined their healing processes. Sooner or later, they began to realize that the relief it promised was hollow; they could not deny that they continued to suffer emotionally.

My answer to the fellow survivor of trauma who questioned the picture on my wall was, "Because it happened." From the moment I hung it I began to use the picture as a gauge to help me gain a sense of where other survivors might be in the healing process and whether or not they were stuck in denial or in any other stage of trauma or grief. As a therapeutic device, it helped me guide them from where they were in any particular moment in time. Several months after I began using the picture in this way, Alicia, another World Trade Center survivor commented, "I don't think I could hang a picture of the event on my walls. I guess I want to pretend it never happened."

The picture served a purpose almost like that of Exposure Therapy, a psychotherapy treatment during which people are exposed to the objects or situations they fear or that have diminished their qualities of life. Exposure therapy inhibits the denial and avoidance that ultimately feeds the anxiety attached to the feared situation or thing. In seeing the picture and knowing of my own trauma, however, other survivors are given an option of whether or not to participate in this sort of exposure, by simply shifting their eyes or moving their chairs. I carefully observed how the person looked at the picture, which demonstrated and clearly reflected the normal sadness generated by such a potent symbol of trauma. The mere verbalization of that sadness became a small indicator that they were moving through the process of healing. On the other hand, if the person avoided the picture, looking away quickly or shifting his or her chair so as not to acknowledge the trauma symbolically, I tried to soothe and reassure them, but also to gently guide the person past the denial this behavior exposed.

Several people I've talked to could not look at the picture at all. Therese, a fifty-six-year-old mother, wife, grandmother and avid dancer, speaks of September 11th,

At 7:30, I arrived at work, settled in and rushed to complete a statistical assignment for one of my company's divisions. At 8:46, I heard a crashing, rumbling sound and the Tower seemed to sway. I immediately hit the floor thinking it was an earthquake. The sounds got louder and all I could do was pray that this would all end in a matter of seconds. I remembered thinking that what I was hearing and feeling were far different from the sounds and movements at the time of the 1993 bombing.

As I waited, I heard people screaming around me but it did not register in my mind how severe the situation was until it felt as though the building would continue to sway out of control, then snap, at which point we would all wind up in the Hudson River. Still under my desk, I began shaking uncontrollably until I heard my boss calling my name. He told me that we had been hit and must evacuate immediately. I quickly headed to the staircase. The walk down felt endless.

When we finally exited the building, I looked back and up at the towers, by then engulfed in flames. My heart dropped. I screamed and then cried. Shakily, I walked all the way to Canal Street. I was lucky to get a train to Pennsylvania Station, but when I arrived all trains were cancelled. Again, I began to shake uncontrollably and I ran out of the terminal. I feared that the same exact thing might happen at the train station and I didn't want to be trapped there. I found myself in a daze, walking downtown until I realized the smoke was coming in my direction. I turned around and headed back in the direction I had come. I finally got through to my husband and at that point I heard someone say that both towers had fallen. When I heard this news, I completely lost it. I went into shock and then denial. I couldn't believe it. I walked and walked until I came upon a church. I went into the church office and stayed about five hours.

And as the weeks passed, Therese recalled her emotions in the wake of her trauma.

I kept hoping it would all go away, but the reality was setting in despite my wishful thinking. People were lost. People were dead. I couldn't cry anymore. I couldn't sleep. The movement of the building, the visual sights, the screaming and yelling all played in my head over and over again. I heard planes and crackling sounds all night long. I became intensely afraid to move. The nights became endless. I couldn't even think of traveling to work, getting on the railroad or being in a tunnel. I couldn't tolerate the idea of being confined anywhere outside my home. I felt I needed to see outside at all times. I wouldn't leave my house.

When Therese was confronted with the picture in my office, her eyes quickly darted away. Moments later, she moved her chair and shifted her body so as to obliterate any chance of even an accidental glance in its direction. In reflecting on her reaction, it seemed that the only control she felt she could exert on her trauma was avoidance and denial. *I'll pretend its not there*, her body language and behavior strongly suggested. As we talked, she admitted that at work she expended a great amount of energy avoiding any reminders of that day. She recalled that she often "sat and remembered the construction of the buildings and could not fathom that they were now gone." As on the day of the attack, she found herself figuratively and symbolically under her desk, avoiding the horror which had unfolded before her and its aftermath.

In our sessions, I guided her through some of the difficult stages of trauma she was experiencing, explained they were common and we talked of the normality of her initial reactions and her response in the immediate aftermath. Then we created a scenario in which she could begin to regain a sense of control while facing the fears and anxiety that were keeping her stuck in the stages of denial and avoidance. We used the real-life upcoming situation of the relocation of her department to an office building she had never seen. We decided that one way to gain a measure of control was to visit the building in advance of her move and to use the pending visit to decide beforehand how she would cope. I asked her to write down her emotions after the visit to help her face some of those feelings that she was actively avoiding. She accepted the challenge and thus began walking her path away from denial and avoidance to one of acknowledgment and healing.

For Corki, the shock of the attack of September 11th, overwhelmed her ability to even acknowledge that such a violent experience occurred. As she recalls,

> I heard a very, very loud noise and panicked. A coworker kept saying to me, "Let's go. Let's go," but I couldn't move. I was filled with fear. Finally, I followed her to the staircase, which was very, very hot. Sweating, I took off my jacket and threw it to another employee. Some time later, I again stopped dead in my tracks, consumed again with fear. I thought I was going to die.
>
> Later, I was taken to a local hospital, because I was unable to breathe or walk. I was totally out of it.

As her world turned upside down, Corki literally closed her eyes. She froze and was utterly unable to think or act. She became like a deer paralyzed by the lights of an oncoming vehicle. Her terror was an anesthetic, shutting her down. Trauma had become encoded in her mind but she could not interpret the sights, sounds and smells in any rational form. She faced death by paralysis and may have perished had it not been for others around her who became her protectors in the absence of her ability to do so for herself. Forced to continue down the stairs, she was pulled from the brink of possible death to where she now stands in the aftermath.

She too could not look at the picture on my office wall or name her trauma. She seemed to be holding fiercely to a muted innocence, resolutely determined that the attack of September 11th would not take away her beliefs about "safety" and that "all is right with the world." She kept telling herself, *Don't think about it. Just go on and do what you have to do.* Yet she came to me with many symptoms: insomnia, nightmares, poor concentration, unhealthy eating habits and was startled by the slightest sound. Her work performance was deteriorating and her symptoms were still increasing.

Despite her obviously strong reactions to the trauma, she could not move beyond the denial stage. She turned her head when a visual reminder suddenly came into view. She closed her ears when those around her spoke of anything that reminded her of that day. As she noted, "I kept telling myself that it was all temporary and that things would go back to the way they were before." Despite her conscious and unconscious attempts at denial, she was constantly anxious and frightened. Even if the mind was not willing, her body let her know that she had been devastated.

Finally, she made her first tenuous step toward acknowledgement; she met with me to say that she was in emotional pain. "From what?" I inquired.

Her eyes welled with tears as she replied, "For all the friends I lost, for the place I worked and those who are leaving because they can't stand the reminders." With agony in her voice she said, "I cannot escape loss."

I acknowledged how hard it is to accept traumatic events, because they are so far outside the scope of our daily experiences. I talked with her about the effects of trauma on the body and mind. I told her how she, as other survivors have done, could move gently toward healing and recovery. The reality of her experience could not be denied if she was ever to heal.

We discussed how she might gradually impel denial to take a back seat and how, by learning to cope with her anxiety, she could begin to experience her grief in small doses. We talked about how she should give herself emotional breaks such as pleasant walks, exercise, soothing music or comedy shows in order to help fortify herself during the healing process.

These are ways you too can aid your progress along the difficult, winding road to recovery. Remember to be gentle and patient with yourself as you take these steps.

Chapter 4 Resilience Tips

- Healing is a gradual process.
- You have to move from one small step to the next in order to recover.
- Denial is not ALL bad. It is a common phase of grief and loss and can allow you to take short breaks from your pain and suffering. However, PERSISTENT denial can stall the healing process.
- Distraction is a healthier alternative to prolonged denial. It allows you to "forget" about the situation for short periods of time while allowing your body and mind to replenish.
- Attack denial in small stages. For instance, allow yourself to act incrementally on an aspect of your loss (e.g., visit a place that does not hold intense memories but is a small part of that loss). Write down what you feel. Begin by doing this one day of the week.
- Take emotional breaks along the path to recovery: physical exercise, listening to soothing music, engaging in hobbies and doing anything that can bring tiny bits of laughter.

EXERCISE

Avoidance can be described as the tendency to move away from cues that create an anxious reaction. When faced with a traumatic event, you may find yourself avoiding cues that remind you of your ordeal. Avoidance behavior may also become generalized and result in a phobic response to numerous cues. Below are various ways in which people avoid traumatic event.

Check all that apply to you and add any other avoidance behaviors that you have experienced since the event.

_____ Strong wish that you will "wake up" and realize it was a bad dream

_____ Avoid thinking about the event

_____ Avoid talking about the event

_____ Avoid acknowledging the event ever happened

_____ Avoid people, places, and things connected with the event

_____ Isolating self from family and friends

_____ Afraid to return to normal daily activities

_____ Feeling panicky when in situations or environments similar to or related to event

_____ Other: _____

If you checked three or more items, try one or more of the following exercises:
   • Try writing down the chain of events leading to the traumatic event.
   • Ask someone who also was there what he or she experienced.
   • Develop a gradual desensitization plan:
      1. Master relaxation techniques including deep breathing, imagery, meditation, muscle relaxation, etc.
      2. Practice selected relaxation technique.
      3. Make a list of at least ten anxiety-producing behaviors

ranked from least to most anxiety provoking.

4. Then, go down your list and imagine carrying out each step, one at a time. Go back and practice **imagining** the previous step if the current step is too anxiety provoking. Or break the current step into two or more easier steps.

5. Pick the least threatening step and follow-through on it **behaviorally** until you are able to carry out each step on your list.

•Use coping statements like "This feeling will pass and I'll be okay."

Chapter 5

Hopelessness and Helplessness:
Trauma and Suicide

For some survivors of a life-altering event or series of events, on the opposite side of denial can lay relentless hopelessness and helplessness. Individuals who feel this way have a sense of futility at not being able to alleviate pain that is both psychic and physical. This creates a sense of worthlessness. It becomes one of the defining aspects of their anguish. Symptoms of depression also contribute to and drive such feelings of worthlessness, hopelessness and helplessness. They can sap self-esteem and energy, so much so that mental fogginess, sleep disturbances and confusion, among other symptoms, may be present.

Traumatic events, with their varying intensities of cognitive, behavioral and emotional aftereffects, may unfortunately lead some survivors to seriously contemplate and plan suicide. When this level of despair emerges, the roadmap to recovery for these individuals often calls for first admitting them into monitored hospital settings where they can be placed on suicide watch. Family members or friends cannot protect vulnerable potential suicides twenty-four hours per day. Hospitalization at such critical times provides around-the-clock supervision and eliminates the means for suicide completion. Although it's often difficult to accept the need for intervention at this level, a proactive approach to protecting despondent people from suicide may be necessary in order to allow them to live through such painful contemplation while offering them opportunities to seek life-affirming solutions to their ordeals.

In my clinical experience with trauma survivors who were suicidal at one point in their lives, the conditions that led them down the path to contemplating suicide were both an inability to experience a sense of self-efficacy and an incapacity to envision other problem-solving avenues. Some described feeling as if they were in completely dark tunnels, bottomless darkness that invaded every cell of their bodies. Others spoke of feeling all-consuming despair that chipped away at their very cores until they lost themselves in desperation's clutches. Such despair was so pervasive that these survivors experienced no relief. Feelings of emptiness, anguish and psychic pain overwhelmed them day and night. One survivor told me that her emotional pain was so unrelenting that it tormented her even in her dreams. Other trauma survivors spoke with me about feeling that the misery in their lives and their failure to relieve the pain led them to conclude that relief was unattainable. Seeking solace from unremitting pain, they viewed suicide as a final yet desperate attempt to attain emotional peace. Others talked of feeling the loss of a suddenly deceased loved one so intensely that their wish to join the deceased overrode any desire to live without them. Just as there are countless traumatic events, there are countless reasons that a person may consider suicide rather than continue living in the aftermath of trauma.

However, those who seriously contemplate suicide frequently exhibit intense hopelessness, loss of self-confidence, absent self-esteem and feelings of worthlessness. This renders them extremely vulnerable to the idea of self-destruction. Certain detrimental social factors in such individuals' lives (loss of social networks, family estrangement, financial burdens) may also lead them to agonize about situations where suicide seems justified. In essence, suicidality is typically a dynamic interaction between emotions such as helplessness, sensations like rapid heart rate, decreased libido, nausea, feelings of hopeless expectations and limited social supports. When extreme distress is felt in more than one area, I have found that for some the potential for suicide completion is heightened. For these individuals early professional attention and intervention usually are critically necessary to help mitigate pain and suffering.

When confronted with a person who is seriously contemplating suicide, many people may ask themselves, *What could be so awful that one would consider suicide the solution?* This is a question that is extremely hard, if not impossible, to answer if the person posing the question has never felt indescribably hopeless about life and completely helpless to change his or her circumstances.

While most of us cannot imagine any life experience that would lead to thoughts of suicide, they are a reality for a growing number of people and the act itself is attempted by many on a daily basis. In fact, today suicidal deaths outnumbers homicide deaths by five to three. In 2000, suicide was the eleventh leading cause of death in the United States and the third leading cause of death among people fifteen to twenty-four years old. Young people in the fifteen to twenty-four age group are also susceptible to suicide "contagion." Suicide contagion is the resultant increase in suicide and suicidal behaviors that occurs after exposure to suicide within the family, peer group or exposure to media reports of suicide. In addition, research indicates that for each completed suicide there are approximately eight to twenty-five attempted suicides. This is why all indicators of suicidal ideation must be taken seriously. It is vitally important to recognize and understand these signs and symptoms in order to protect one's self, loved ones and others who may, at some time, feel such searing anguish.

Suicide Signs and Symptoms

One important signal to be aware of is that a despairing person often moves along a continuum in increasing severity. From one stage to the next, the potential for suicide completion becomes more and more serious. Therefore, it is best that the person suffering from suicidal feelings and thoughts seek or is provided with professional help before it is too late. In my practice, I have seen individuals who spoke to family and/or me of having thoughts of suicide and who used phrases such as "I wish I was dead" or "It would be better if I was not around." Though these phrases are passive and those who only verbalize death wishes (stage one) are less likely to engage in suicidal behavior, it is nonetheless necessary to take immediate professional steps to help such individuals seek and act on life-affirming solutions to their problems rather than progress to the next stage.

The second stage, contemplation, is a more serious stage on the continuum of suicidality. This stage strongly suggests that the individual has rejected or can no longer envision life-affirming solutions and is actively engaging in thoughts of ending his or her life. Trauma survivors who reach this stage generally require intense professional supervision and hospitalization. When sufferers are at this juncture they are more likely to actively plan their suicide. This stage of suicide contemplation therefore signals increasing hopelessness.

Planning, or stage three, is often accompanied by destructive behaviors such as self-imposed isolation from family and friends, abandonment of future planning, giving away one's possessions, writing one's will or penning a suicide note. This is an emergency. Hospitalization is imperative in such cases.

Unfortunately, some trauma survivors do attempt and complete suicides. Adolescents in particular are at high risk, especially following traumatic events where a parent, sibling or friend has committed suicide. Factors such as substance or alcohol abuse, genetics (such as family history of suicide completion or family history of mental illness), the inability to control impulses, physiology (decreased levels of serotonin in the brain, a neurochemical strongly implicated in depression) and, in some cases, auditory hallucinations, may also play roles in suicide attempts and completions.

Trauma and the Wish for Relief

Because of such individualized factors as personality characteristics, presence of alcohol or substance abuse and deepening depression, interventions need to be tailored to the specific needs of the suicidal person in order to manage suicidal risk. In the aftermath of her trauma, one of the sufferers, Mara, found herself constantly thinking about suicide. Then one day she said to me, "Live or die? It doesn't matter to me."

Mara talked with me about the dark tunnel of hopelessness in which she felt trapped. When I asked her about her reasons for feeling suicidal, she told me that the world was too dangerous and that she was terribly afraid. She said that she desired relief from a multitude of fears that seemed to multiply each day, but that she had not thought about suicide beyond the wish that, "Sometimes I hope that I will just not wake up in the morning." I asked her about any past or current thoughts or behaviors that might lead her beyond simple thoughts about suicide and nearer to actual suicidal intent. She denied that she felt any such intent. She also denied any alcohol or substance abuse or that she had plans to commit suicide. She wanted death to happen passively, with no effort on her part.

As she led me further into her world of despondency, we began to talk about how she might move away from such reflections and, instead, move toward healing.

"You are experiencing not only tremendous anguish but intense fear," I reflected. "It must feel harder and harder to bear these burdens as each day passes. I know your need for relief must seem almost unbearable," I said as I leaned towards her sympathetically.

Mara nodded. "Yes. I want to feel better. I'm tired of it all," she told me.

"Let me share some other solutions that could give you relief," I said. We began to explore ways she could decrease her heightened levels of depression and anxiety. We talked about symptom management techniques and ways Mara could comfort herself. We also discussed how she could increase her coping and problem-solving skills. These discussions centered on garnering the support of social networks and community resources. We decided that she could begin to rebuild her sense of self-mastery by completing at least one task a day and building upon that task until self-confidence and feelings of control surfaced.

Equally importantly, we worked to recapture the coping strengths within that were currently hidden from her. We also discussed any adaptive, life-affirming beliefs and values, including issues of spirituality, that had been available to her before her trauma. We talked about strategies she used in the past to successfully manage states of anxiety and depression. We explored future goals and plans she held that had become clouded by her depression and fears. We decided that medication would also offer temporary relief while we worked on more permanent ones and we talked about the good things in her life and those who needed her, including her ten-year-old daughter. Through talk and action, Mara began to see that there were not only strengths within her, but that there were also alternatives to dealing with her trauma that she had not yet considered or tried. In effect, Mara regained hope.

Unlike Mara, the potential for suicide in Carol, another of my clients, was more troubling as she demonstrated a propensity for impulsive behavior and agitation. Given her tendency toward impulsiveness, the more lethal suicide stages of intent, plan and attempt could overlap each other in rapid succession. In Carol's case, I regarded any self-destructive behavior as potentially lethal. Therefore, I introduced a plan for tight structure in her life and was on the lookout for any behaviors that were reckless or self-destructive.

In one session Carol casually mentioned that she had had unprotected sex with a stranger the night before, behavior that was obviously self-destructive and dangerous. I also knew Carol as being a person with strong propensities toward an initial interpersonal over-involvement followed by emotional rejection. For Carol, this emotional seesaw typically manifested itself in her fear of being betrayed and the belief that if given the opportunity people would be hurtful toward her. These and other factors contributed to her experience of depressive symptoms. I felt that she seemed to be setting herself up for another depressive episode and for further harm to herself. We had to explore this situation in-depth to avert a catastrophe.

"Why is it that you mention such clearly dangerous behavior in such a casual manner?" I asked.

"Well, it was a one-night stand. You can't get any more casual than that," she replied, jokingly.

"Carol," I said in a concerned tone, "you are joking about something that is potentially life-threatening. Let's talk instead about the possible negative consequences to the health and well-being of a person who has unprotected sex with a stranger. What risks were there that the act could have produced violent or tragic results?"

"Well, he could have killed me or he might have had a sexually transmitted disease," she said. "He could have even raped me."

Carol was a survivor of childhood sexual abuse. Her behavior raised issues of "repetition in the service of trauma mastery," and given her history, it seemed likely that more self-destructive and ultimately dangerous sexual behavior could emerge. While Carol did not have a prior history of suicide ideation, intent, plans or attempts, her self-destructive behavior could be construed as an indirect attempt (putting herself in situations where she could be infected with a disease and/or killed). Carol and I talked about her behavior in the context of her history of sexual abuse. We laid the groundwork for viewing her actions in this light and at the same time, worked to change such impulsive and self-destructive behaviors.

From then on, each time Carol acted on any self-destructive behavior, I searched with her for the potential consequences of such behavior and how she might act to correct the behavior. Carol made an

appointment with her gynecologist and was tested for sexually transmitted diseases. In addition, she promised me that she would stop having unprotected sex. Instead, she agreed to learn strategies to limit
impulsive behaviors, including ways she could decrease her heightened levels of agitation through techniques that might bring her solace
and comfort. I highlighted and encouraged her to practice more adaptive behavior, including utilizing the healthy coping and problem-solving skills she already possessed. Over time, Carol eventually began to
believe that she deserved much more than that brought about by her
destructive behavior.

Other Avenues to Life-affirming Behavior

Trauma can dramatically alter people's lives and social supports. When
it occurs, those affected may lose hope either because they themselves
have been severely damaged or lost loved ones. Suicidal thoughts or
actions may surface. If they do, those who see a loved one or friend in
such a position must accept suicide as a real possibility and, despite our
own personal moral, religious or spiritual views, make every effort to
help the person who may be considering such a path.

Social and community support services, including hospitalization, are critical interventions for those who are considering suicide. Focused attention on the planning and preparation for suicide, a
low level of impulse control and means to suicide (e.g., having access
to a gun) are all indicators for hospitalization. Prior suicide attempts
or behavior and thoughts associated with intent are also strong indicators that hospitalization is necessary.

Fortunately, the majority of trauma survivors do not reach the
point at which suicide becomes a viable option to them. Many learn to
manage the intense emotional distress and other related responses to the
traumatic events they've suffered. Interpersonal support and other
resources that facilitate coping will help many survivors as they attempt
to move toward life renewal. Even those who experience prolonged suffering often maintain some level of hope and some belief in their ability
to successfully cope with adversity. While many moving through the
early and middle stages of trauma feel unlike others who have not dealt
with trauma, they nonetheless begin to reflect on what was lost in order
to regain their equilibrium and thereby ultimately embrace the healing
path.

If you consider suicide at any point in your life, please reach out for professional help in order to begin healing and find the positive in your future. For in your pain lies wisdom, a wisdom that comes into being when you emerge from your deep pool of sorrow. You, like many others who have suffered terrible traumas, can trust in your inherent ability to embrace life and begin the process of learning to live again.

Chapter 5 Resilience Tips

- After suffering trauma, if you are having thoughts of dying or killing yourself, recognize that you are most likely suffering from depression—a treatable condition. Please, realize that depression does end and that you can heal from your suffering, grief and loss. Seek professional help immediately or call 911.
- Recognize that you may also be experiencing post-traumatic stress symptoms that are also treatable. Mental health professionals can help. Seek help immediately or call 911.
- Detoxify your home. Flush old medication down the toilet, remove firearms, knives and other lethal weapons.
- Avoid self-medication including alcohol, illegal drugs and inappropriate use of prescription drugs.
- Seek treatment for addictive behavior.
- Take anti-depressant medication.
- Talk to someone you trust who will listen with compassion to your feelings.
- Think about the people in your life for whom you care and who care for you. Make an agreement to call them if you feel suicidal.
- Even if you want to be alone, seek the presence of others if you are having suicidal thoughts.
- Seek a physically and emotionally safe environment.
- Realize that you are not alone. Get support.

EXERCISE

Beliefs and attitudes are the value judgments and expectations that influence our reactions to people and situations. Beliefs and attitudes are typically formed by our culture, our family upbringing, and also developed on the basis of our adult experiences. Below are some of the more common core beliefs that people may hold. Check those that you believe. Add any belief you hold that is not listed. Then, rate each belief on a scale of 1 through 7, with 7 being the most strongly held.

	BELIEF	SCORE
____	If you treat people fairly, they should treat you in the same way.	____
____	When something bad happens to you, it means you were "bad" in the past.	____
____	Bad things should not happen to good people.	____
____	Justice always prevails.	____
____	People never change.	____
____	When things are going well, it's just a matter of time before things go "wrong."	____
____	It's not good to try new things because you may fail.	____
____	It's always good to go with what everyone around. you is doing.	____
____	We have no control over what happens to us.	____
____	It's always best to get the approval of others around you.	____
____	Once something affects your life in a major way, it always will.	____
____	OTHER _____	____

It is very difficult to think of anything that is *always* true. By the same token, beliefs or attitude that include words like "should," "always" or "never" are likely to cause distress and disappointment to the believer. To help you gain a more balanced perspective of yourself, others and the world around you, answer the following questions for any of the above beliefs in which you scored three or higher:

CHALLENGING BELIEFS

1. With an objective mind and considering all of my life experiences, what is the evidence that this belief is ALWAYS true?

2. Does this belief consider both positive and negative aspects of the issue?

3. Is this a belief I developed based on my life experiences or is it a belief developed when growing up?

4. Is this belief helpful to my peace of mind and well-being?

Chapter 6

Loss of Innocence:
The Search for an Expanded Worldview

Experiencing trauma can impart, among other things, lessons about fear, loss and grief. Yet, before survivors are ready to embrace recovery and solidly step on the healing path, trauma teaches yet another important lesson—that it can deflate the very thing that defines a survivor's life, that is, one's core belief systems. No matter from what source trauma originates, sexual abuse in childhood, physical violence, rape, natural or man-made disaster or the unexpected loss of a loved one, trauma frequently leads survivors to question their basic beliefs and attitudes. In general, survivors' questions span the spectrum from beliefs about trust in others to their faith in God. This conflict between trauma and one's belief system can be highly charged, as most of us have internalized comfortable credos about reality so as to pragmatically limit fear and anxiety in our daily lives. Just as earlier stages of trauma and its aftermath often are devastating to survivors, changes in core basic belief systems also can be highly distressing.

When we are untouched by tragedy, our view of the world normally assumes dimensions of safety and control. There is an implied innocence inherent in such an assumption. Typically secure in our surroundings, we go year-to-year, decade-to-decade feeling that these things are fixed and undeniable. Some think of the world as benevolent and most often, at least when young, think of ourselves as fairly invincible. Prior to being faced with tragedy, one may have held fiercely to the anxiety-reducing belief that certain family members would be around for support throughout one's lifetime. One may have believed that the physical disability that now limits his or her life could only happen to someone else. Perhaps one held the belief that natural disasters such as earthquakes, floods or tornadoes would never destroy one's home. Another belief that may be challenged is that a family member would never intentionally inflict harm.

When adversity strikes, traumatic reactions can suddenly become overpowering and anguish no longer a concept to be viewed objectively from a safe distance. The grief that is tragedy's twin is no longer academic or abstract. Life-altering events lead the survivor to initially internalize the loss while beliefs and attitudes about the self and the world are thrown off-kilter. During this period of shock, the survivor's internal terrain can become an intense and tortured place.

The individual elements of the trauma that intimately touches a person causes that person to question the sanctity of his or her assumptions about the world. In essence, whatever our prior beliefs, trauma challenges and changes, initial trauma can be laced with the compounding trauma of a world turned upside-down, where loss of safety and loss of meaning become invisible wounds.

Trauma as "Unfair"

Over the years, talking to survivors confronted with different adversities, I have found that some at first repress or do not want to discuss the impact of their trauma on their lives. However, as trust was established I found that many questioned the manners in which they had previously lived their lives, while simultaneously reevaluating global beliefs about themselves and others. Such considerations often revolved around the previously unchallenged and strongly held beliefs about "justice in the world," "trust in mankind" and "trust in the self."

Corki, a September 11th survivor, came to view life as having an added dimension of somber unfairness. "The event changed my environment and my friendships. My whole world changed!" she said with strong conviction. I have found that like Corki, other survivors frequently articulate life's "unfairness." Ultimately forced to acknowledge that there are no true guarantees in life, these survivors recognize that their specific calamity now resides within their individual reality and that prior tragic events are not a shield from even greater future traumas. Furthermore, that which was once seen as the tapestry of their life, to which previously held beliefs bound the self to the self and others, can become unglued in seconds. Inevitably, such questioning causes their core beliefs about themselves and the world to fragment and survivors often find themselves lost. They search to find physical, mental and spiritual realms of comfort.

The survivors I followed have shared that at such points their expectations about themselves and the world spiraled downward. They lost their sense of personal empowerment and their relationship to others often deteriorated. Some described this as finding themselves in a forest or an isolated desert. It was as if the trauma with its assault on their belief systems, left them frozen in time with little self-identity. When the survivor was left in this state for a period of time, the trauma could then cause protracted physical, emotional and spiritual damage, depleting the individual's self-confidence and causing the person to feel there was no meaning in daily events. This mode of being undermined these survivors' potential and limited their interpersonal relationships.

Trauma and Existential Anxiety

Like these survivors, if you are a trauma sufferer you may have felt your self-assurance chipping away and your anxiety centered on whether you can sustain the fortitude necessary to regain your sense of self and relationships with others. In contrast to the actual tragedy, where issues of surviving was the primary consideration and preceded any other consideration, in the act of further processing trauma, issues concerning the survivor's self-identity and essence take center stage. Often as a byproduct of trauma, a survivor's personal substance no longer feels assured, perceptions of the self became fuzzy and anxiety about one's true character emerges.

I have learned that at this critical juncture it is essential for you and other survivors to reflect on your prior assumptions before you can begin your journey toward a rebalanced perspective of yourself and the world around you.

Greg, who experienced a workplace shooting, confided with articulated guilt and shame, that in his period of self-doubt he was haunted by the thought: *I can't do this job anymore.* He was expressing a sense of lost identity, as prior to his ordeal he had felt that his career defined him. Although I reassured him of the validity of his feelings, I have found that survivors such as Greg remain anxious until affirmation, clarity of self and purpose become subjectively more transparent. Although your own progress toward this goal will be unique, know that the paths others have trod can lend light to your journey.

Janet, whose father was a murder victim, said,"I believed that my dad would live forever. I thought that his strength would stave off every obstacle life put in his path. I believed nothing could bring him down." Janet's deeply held beliefs about her father's invincibility left her floating in a state of existential anxiety.

She asked herself, *If her father could be brought down, couldn't everyone?*

As we worked through her bereavement we also discussed existential issues of death and meaningless. It became apparent that Janet was struggling with the thought that if her father could die so abruptly, life may ultimately be meaningless. Beyond reconciling herself to her father's death, Janet's healing task was also to pursue purpose and meaning in her own life. Others I have worked with have voiced their needs to believe not only that their lost loved ones' lives were meaningful, but their own still are. Periods of intense introspection occurred as these survivors became aware of and then articulated what was most important to them in general and how their individual conceptions of meaningfulness filtered outward to those around them. In every case I have found that one of the most important healing steps of the journey is for the individuals to look inward in ways previously uncharted in search of a more resilient identification of their essential beings. You too may find this step important, so that you can have a new vision of the self you still can be.

In addition to concerns about the self and meaningfulness, issues of personal death, responsibility, freedom and guilt coming to the foreground for these survivors can also be defined as an existential anxiety. Many of those with whom I have worked who survived disasters were particularly concerned about existential survivor guilt, questioning why they had lived while others had not, as well as the meaning of their survival. Some even verbalized the wish to change places with deceased loved ones.

Survivor guilt in such cases seems not only to address emotional and intellectual aspects of guilt but also include other anxiety issues. These issues often included concerns about one's own pending death and one's ultimate life purpose. However, be reassured that through meditation, counseling and healing measures, this period of self-doubt can be finite. As you and other survivors begin to heal, survivor guilt can give way to understanding and acceptance of reality. One way to begin this healing is to keep in mind while on your own search for an expanded worldview that there are many survivors who have successfully completed this aspect of their journeys. Their journeys may lead you to embark on your own healing journey.

For example, like Bob, you may feel the cherished beliefs you held and once deemed to be true haunt you and undermine your mental and physical well-being. As he stated, "Intellectually, we all are aware that bad things happen to people. But in our hearts we also believe that bad things cannot happen to us." Despite the reality of his trauma, clinging to the belief that bad things could not happen to him held Bob captive. Emotionally, he fought against reality and in the process diminished his ability to recover. "I can't seem to get back to normal," he told me. "The doctors keep telling me that I should be further along in my recovery, yet I'm still in a lot of pain and I've been depressed since this happened."

Over a period of time we discussed Bob's mindset. "It is certainly sometimes difficult to believe grave misfortune has occurred in your life even when it's staring you in the face," I said.

"It sure is hard to believe! The question of how could this happen comes to my mind every single day," he confided.

Bob was physically and emotionally frozen and could not moved forward very far on his healing path. I asked Bob to consider ways he might care for himself in this agonized state, despite his disbelief. "Think like a child for a few moments and believe that if you wish it so, it will be so. Assume no boundaries and let your imagination soar," I suggested. In asking him to use his imagination, I also stipulated that he view his situation as an opportunity to perhaps engage in an activity he enjoyed but rarely in the past made time to do.

Bob slowly began to use his imagination to face his dilemma. As we continued to work together, he was eventually able to let go of his fierce rejection of the reality of his trauma. Several weeks later, he told me, "You know, one day I was thinking about what you said about this time being an opportunity to do things I never make time for but that I enjoy," he confided. "I always loved old diesel trains. So, that afternoon I went to the library and I took out some books on trains. Although, at first I couldn't read more than a page or two, I have been enjoying them immensely ever since. I feel so much better and I see myself improving physically too."

By accepting the reality of his situation and using his adversity as an opportunity, Bob began to heal.

Carol's struggle illuminates some of the dynamics of trauma. When one has been sexually abused as a child, as an adult, in order to move forward, one must discover a more balanced and integrated view of self and others that expands and moves beyond these traumas. Early on in treatment, Carol asked me, "How can a person succeed in life if she never received a foundation of love from her mother?"

I reflected on her words for a few moments then replied, "Let's first imagine what that person who was harmed so much as a child might feel and then let's imagine how that person with those feelings could still succeed."

Prior to therapy, Carol believed that her childhood trauma had forever branded her. The life she felt condemned to live, one of dissatisfaction and unsuccessful endeavor, had become a self-fulfilling prophecy. Given her young age and the circumstances at the time she suffered from ritual sexual abuse, Carol's trauma impacted heavily upon her personality development and character structure. In order to counteract this early personality impoverishment, I slowly engaged her in a process of seeking the potential messages of self-awareness and personal growth that still were within her despite her pain. I knew a more positive sense of self could eventually be realized. As she began to trust me more fully, Carol and I began to observe and articulate her steadfast beliefs, feelings and thoughts more closely. She then began to imagine possibilities as we discussed ways she could transcend her trauma, seeking to find a richer and more fulfilling state of being. This imaginative exercise is one you too can emulate if you are emotionally stuck in a trauma you suffered long ago.

First find a quiet place. Then write down what you feel when you remember your past hurt. Let out all you may have been keeping hidden. Now spend some time thinking and write down a list of things to do which, despite the past, could lead to fulfillment. For some, this could be getting counseling, helping others who have suffered similar injuries or finding a satisfying career or other new gratification.

Locating the Self after a Traumatic Experience

Survivors need to accept that they cannot expand themselves and their worldviews overnight. Suddenly accosted by tragedy, we are more likely to fall back on that which has worked in the past even if logically we know that a different path needs to be taken. As we look toward the future, we must expect that we will also glimpse what lies behind us. When this happens we grieve for what was familiar to us. Yet if we are to move forward, we must realize that while we might try to recapture the comfortable and the familiar, our adversity compels us to see that it is no longer possible.

Sometimes, we even feel that we are finally recapturing who we once were. Then, trauma drifts us along to another side of itself and we may begin to feel lost. As I counseled them, I frequently saw World Trade Center survivors and stricken families in tears, their faces showing anguish, grief and loss. Some hyperventilated, others shook uncontrollably and still others moaned, rocking their bodies so as to soothe themselves. Their sobs, at times, seemed never-ending. They spoke of how the juxtaposition of grief and trauma against their pre-trauma selves created an atmosphere where their lives now seemed out of order. Some struggled to integrate these incongruous demands within the functions of their daily lives, as it was inconceivable to many how they could find themselves too distraught to perform their normal daily tasks. When their concentration failed and anxiety drained them emotionally, doing those mundane things that were normally second nature to them suffered as well. Often they criticized themselves; they articulated the dissatisfaction they felt at not being able to perform at their pre-trauma level. They felt they were disappointing family, friends, supervisors, coworkers and, most importantly, themselves.

Emotional First Aid

For any survivor to believe that he or she can no longer do those things that were normally second nature causes painful feelings. Be aware that such feelings are not abnormal. You are not alone. Trauma can render any survivor temporarily helpless and overwhelmed in emotional, physical, spiritual and mental spheres. Trauma can cause survivors' ordinary defenses and coping mechanisms to fail. When you feel such painful emotions, it is important to have one-on-one discussions with close friends, family members, therapists and clergy-people who can empathize and impress upon you the importance of being gentle with yourself in this time of self-restoration rather than complicating the healing process by being self-critical and judgmental.

In working with survivors of tragedy who are operating in self-critical modes, I felt it vital to provide a soothing and comforting balm of anti-demoralization. I provide "containment" of such self-critical tendencies, a holding space that will allow survivors the opportunity to experience more flexibility in their thinking, even in the midst of emotional turmoil. To do this I try to create the space for both expert assistance and coaching by prioritizing the fostering of emotional safety. It is very important that you as a survivor feel safe with someone with whom you can share your feelings. Rather than using self-critical defenses, I seek to offer the survivors I work with an intervention that will allow for the active experience and, more importantly, acceptance of all levels of awareness in a therapeutically safe environment.

It is essential that you understand that when you feel numb, unable to work or relate to others you care about, it often occurs because of the trauma you have suffered within the context of the trauma you have suffered and is not something that you have brought on yourself. On the practical side, there are survivor skills that reduce the risk of being re-traumatized, including relaxation techniques and strategies for coping. One exercise I suggest which some survivors have found very useful when feeling overwhelmed is to take a time out. Look around, repeat to yourself the names of the colors in a room or count out the change in your pocket.

Another strategy is to discover your triggers and find ways to cope with them. Use terms like "at that time" and "when it happened" in order to help you differentiate between then and the here-and-now. I have found that these simple phrases help survivors stay oriented in the present.

The survivors I see in private practice are aided by psychological first aid so they can begin to heal. Hopefully, by reading in this book some of these accounts and interventions you may feel a resonance with your own situation and may re-think feelings in a more healing manner. Remember, in the end, all survivors of trauma need to discover and embrace their individual paths to healing.

Carol, the survivor of sexual abuse that we discussed previously, missed a session near the beginning of treatment. She called a day later, stating that she had decided on impulse to get on an airplane the day before and go to Boston. She was calling me from a hotel. She told me that she did not call her job to tell them she would not be in for work. She also knew that she could not afford to pay the credit card charges she incurred for the plane ticket and in obtaining the hotel room. As she spoke, I quietly reflected back on the few sessions we had had and began formulating a hypothesis that might explain her impulsive behavior.

I recalled that Carol seemed to act as if she was doomed to fail. She appeared to believe that she had been damaged at an early age and therefore there was little purpose in being responsible. I decided that psychological first aid was needed. However, she had to return to New York in order for me to continue to guide her on a healing path. For the moment, I felt I needed to be the benevolent mother she so strongly desired in order to help her become the person she could be.

With "motherly" concern and resolve in my tone, I said, "Carol, you have to get back on an airplane today and return to New York. I will see you in my office tomorrow afternoon." Fortunately, she agreed. When she arrived for her appointment, we began to explore how she could integrate her traumatic experiences rather than fragment them through self-destructive and impulsive behaviors.

As with Carol, I have worked with other survivors who unconsciously acted on aspects of their traumas. Jim, a man who saw a shooting on the subway, developed medically inexplicable migraine headaches when the prospect of riding the subway seemed likely. Helen, another survivor, fell physically ill on the anniversary of her automobile accident. Margaret suffered from panic attacks whenever she was in a movie theatre, as it reminded her of the sense of confinement she felt after being trapped in an elevator during a fire in her apartment building. Will provoked arguments with his current girlfriend whenever she attempted to hug him. He had been trapped on a derailed commuter train while his previous girlfriend lay dead next to him. It is in these varied trauma states in which survivors struggled before they were able to increase their self-awareness and move forward on healing paths. Their eventual mastery of their trauma indicates that you too can find your own way to recovery despite being stuck in one aspect of your suffering. There is no single way out.

One question stubbornly haunted Liz, a September 11th survivor, after her trauma, *Who am I really? Who is this person now very, very afraid, who is too paralyzed to even help herself?* she agonized. Liz conveyed a wish to better know herself and the desire to move beyond her ordeal. She was, in essence, attempting to relocate her "self" in the glare of her trauma. In working with trauma survivors, my primary task is giving ordinary life back its value and richness and guiding each individual to the re-creation of a worldview that can successfully integrate both the positive and the difficult aspects of his or her life. This goal also is my wish for you.

I hope to empower fellow sufferers to journey on paths to healing in both positive and concrete manners. I have tried to validate and actively reflect on the reactions of those I have counseled. In order to reach this step you must observe and attend to how and what you are thinking and to pay attention to what you are individually feeling. Let us move through your trauma by getting closer to its emotional aspects and farther away from protracted denial or other frozen stages.

In this period, as we discuss and move toward that goal, you must learn to tolerate distress, since by its nature trauma is distressing and therefore each survivor must accept that distress is a facet of trauma that cannot be avoided. Rather than squandering your energy attempting to eradicate the reality of trauma, I encourage you to find value in that which is being felt and revealed in your suffering. Allow difficult emotions and states of being to gently float away as you return to a calmer state.

In the end, healing begins with a level of acceptance and life-affirming renewal. In my own practice I have genuinely engaged in life-affirming dialogue with each survivor with whom I have talked.

Remember, trauma forces many survivors to let go of certain assumptions, sometimes in a previously unimaginable manner, in order to move forward. To do this requires that the survivor take into consideration both past life experiences and life-altering events. Working through the process of trauma seems best achieved when the survivor can be truthful with him or herself about the past and accept the world as it is. Though you will be changed because of the traumatic events you've experienced, the reality of trauma also encompasses other dimensions including an expansion of worldview that can be helpful in transcending the pain of loss. This is the task for all trauma survivors and it is a lesson that survivors must learn so that adversity does not diminish their lives forever. The lesson is, bluntly but meaningfully put, you must learn to live again.

The survivors I have worked with who have successfully traveled their own healing journeys show that people can effectively work to ensure that, though they are impacted, they are not permanently damaged by their prior ordeals or even multiple traumas. As they reach the point of acceptance, they figuratively hold hope in their own hands and explore new life dreams. In essence, it is necessary for each survivor to create future dreams and aspirations so he or she can live life with positive plans for the future.

In my work with trauma survivors, I also strongly stress the resilience of the human spirit. When naturally absent, learned resilience has eased intrinsically painful transitions for sufferers as they move toward healing. One of my goals for you and all who have suffered trauma is to help you move toward a re-adjusted self. I have found that an important first task on the path to healing for all trauma survivors is integration: forming new insights and realizing lessons learned from their ordeals which bring them back into a healthy engagement with daily life. Only then can survivors forge an expanded worldview. In the process, survivors often discover that this expansion additionally includes new imagined passion in their relatedness to themselves and others.

Of course, my own trauma has also caused me to rethink my worldview. My ordeal and its aftermath initially led me to a sense of vulnerability and my imaginings in its wake forced me to tackle fear in order to forge a new comfort zone and to formulate my life's purpose. This may be true for you as well.

In the early stages of my traumatic reaction, I suddenly found myself wondering where "my things" were: the family pictures that were on my office desk, the extra pair of shoes I kept in my desk, the jacket that hung from my office coat rack. The presence of these personal items in my day-to-day life represented a control I believed I had over my environment. I believed if I left an item in my surroundings it should remain where it was left. After September 11th, I struggled with the fact that this was not automatically so. I also struggled with the possibility that I might not live to a ripe old age, dying peacefully in my sleep. My family also was forced to give up the illusion that they were guaranteed I would be around for years to come. For months, following those hours after the collapse of the Twin Towers, when my family had not yet heard from me, their daily "check in" calls were oddly laced with long pauses, as if in those silent moments they were trying to reassure themselves that they were not conversing with an apparition.

Through my own self-reflection, my private practice sessions with trauma victims and in working with hundreds of September 11th survivors and families, I have come to believe that adversity is fundamentally experiential. I feel now that what one does with the experience can be subjectively more important than the event itself. Remember, you must process trauma, become familiar with the effects of the experience instead of fighting it in order to re-establish order, reexamine and retain operative core beliefs and formulate new ones in the face of a changed perspective. Ultimately, it was the discovery of a clearer sense of uniqueness after wandering within the center of adversity that crystallized this transitional period for me and the many survivors I have treated or supported.

Finding New Bearings

In our work together, I have seen slow, dawning recognition occur for scores of survivors of many kinds of trauma. The recognition that their normal way of being in the world has changed caused a realization that they needed to find their bearings in a different world where, among other things, innocence, predictability and invincibility could no longer be assumed. As their healing progressed, they also found positives created by their trauma. One strong positive is the opportunity to learn how to maintain and affirm the spontaneity for life after tragedy strikes.

As survivors stepped more firmly on healing paths, establishing integrated selves and worldviews became the focus. As I worked with these survivors, we began to discuss their lost worldviews, how to regain equilibrium and replace hopelessness with hope and recovery. What emerges for many survivors is life-affirming determination to overcome their despair and to get back on their feet by coping with the emotional, behavioral and physiological pain of adversity.

Hopefully, reading about how other survivors worked through various distressing emotional states after experiencing trauma will inspire you so that you too can and will find your own unique path to healing. Be aware that many of these survivors once felt they were falling apart. However, with time, counsel and self-knowledge they came together. As Steff noted, "I have come to believe that catastrophes by themselves do not lead to positive change. It is the person's ongoing pursuit of positive change that makes permanent positive changes possible."

Chapter 6 Resilience Tips

- In the aftermath of sudden tragedy, you may begin to agonize over a number of your past basic beliefs and attitudes about yourself and the world around you. Some of these beliefs may have been firmly held by you throughout your life. For example, you may have believed that bad things could not really happen to you.
- Postpone major decisions during this period of shock. Recognize that after trauma this questioning period is normal. Do not try to make immediate decisions. Reflect on the beliefs and attitudes that you now are questioning when you are able to think more clearly.
- Acknowledge to yourself that anxiety is common during this turbulent period. When feeling particularly anxious, practice deep breathing, other relaxation techniques or distracting activities.
- Reframe old beliefs and attitudes in a manner that includes new insights into both positive and difficult aspects of life which acknowledge the reality of your loss.
- Remind yourself of the need to move toward a life-affirming healing path. For example, in your own words, try to incorporate this outlook: "Disasters do happen and I may now need to be more cautious. However, I do not need to limit my enjoyment of what remains or the positive things to come."
- Engage in positive actions such as making a list of future goals and ways you plan to realize these goals.
- Explore new or never acted upon aspirations.

EXERCISE

Using the following scale, rate yourself in the areas below:

0 = Not at all
1 = Ocassionally
2 = Sometimes
3 = Often
4 = Always

HYPER-AROUSAL

Hyper-arousal is increased sensory sensitivity that causes one to feel uncomfortable, extra alert and aware of the minutest sounds, vibrations and sights in one's environment. This state is typically accompanied by muscle tension and feelings of restlessness. One is apt to respond in a startled manner to one's environment.

SCORE: _____

If your score is greater than 2, try a few of the following interventions when experiencing hyper-arousal.
- Drink herbal teas.
- Take a bath.
- Meditate.
- Deep breathing.
- Positive self-talk.
- Engage in pleasurable activity or hobby.
- Exercise.
- Pray.

IRRITABILITY

Irritability is a general intolerance or the tendency to be over-sensitive to normal environmental cues or the benign actions of others.

SCORE: _____

If your score is greater than 3, try a few of the following interventions when you feel irritated.
- Determine underlying source of irritability (e.g., fear, grief, etc.)

and, if possible, act constructively to resolve issue.
- Imagine a relaxing scene.
- Relax areas of your body that become tense as a result of your irritation.
- Watch a comedy show.
- Listen to soothing music.

ANGER/RAGE

Anger is feeling hostile toward things or others in your environment. Rage is intense anger. Both anger and rage may be accompanied by angry thoughts, body tension and actions (e.g., yelling, cursing, throwing objects, etc.).

SCORE: _____

If your score is greater than 2, try a few of the following interventions when experiencing anger.
- Determine underlying source of anger/rage (e.g., feeling helpless or powerless to change situation) and, if possible, act constructively to resolve issue.
- Take a walk.
- Do gardening
- Count to ten.

Chapter 7

One Step at a Time:
Embracing the Healing Path

The personal accounts and the charted routes of survivors of trauma highlighted in this book thus far illustrate that though each sufferer's reaction is unique, there are a number of common phases after life-altering events. This commonality is a fabric woven through the lives of each and every trauma survivor. If you are a survivor, I know you have borne witness to the making of this fabric through both poignant and painful renderings. Some survivors move beyond shock and fear within weeks of their ordeals while others remain in this condition for several months or even years. Some quickly shift into the grief phase while others survivors remain in denial for a long period of time. The people I have profiled thus far have shared all of these and other possibilities.

I hope this will be reassuring if you, like many others, are faced with sudden adversity and feel stuck in one aspect of your reaction. For, although trauma indeed comes in many manifestations, fear, rage, shock, horror, denial, uncertainty, terror, helplessness, disgust, powerlessness, shame and grief are often ever-present states of being when unexpectedly confronted with tragedy. If you view your trauma within this framework it will help you to acknowledge as normal the range of emotions you are feeling. As you move toward acceptance, this becomes an important step on your own pathway to recovery. Remember, the possibilities for healing can be as extraordinary as the event itself. I have found and research has shown that those who overcome adversities in their lives move on to become more self-confident. Some even find richer lives and new purposes related to that which had caused such pain. I have observed those who have lost loved ones to drunken drivers later become advocates for anti-drunk driving laws, helping to save the lives of others. I have seen an incest survivor make her life's work helping other incest survivors to move beyond their traumas and a person whose child was killed in an airplane crash become a crusader for airline safety. Whatever the new mission, it may comfort you to know that these survivors have found satisfaction and contentment in lives reconfigured by the tragedy that struck them. You too can experience happiness again and rebuild your life in a fulfilling way. It will be different than the life you had planned in the past, though. Perhaps it will even be better.

Healing Beginnings

To help you along the healing path, it is worthwhile to learn the effects of trauma on the individual and to understand how trauma affects personal development through the life stages of childhood, adolescence, early adulthood and mature adulthood.

As we've discussed, trauma compels the survivor to develop an expanded self in order to reconcile the traumatic events experienced with his or her personality and belief system. Then the person can use already established personal resources or find new ones. It is critical that developmental repair takes place so that the individual does not remain frozen, a state in which avoidance and other deterrents to quality of life become all-encompassing. For instance, in helping Carol face her first trauma, we turned our attention to the early healthy developmental milestones she missed as a result of the sexual abuse she experienced at age eight. This process involves a conscious reexperiencing of the trauma so that the entire experience can be reintegrated. Conscious reexperience, while painful, is necessary in order to halt unconscious negative behaviors and feelings that control the individual. Such behaviors include disassociative feelings, flashbacks and perceptual distortions.

I have found that those survivors who learn and practice skills for coping with trauma are able to avoid or mitigate the potential long-term destructiveness of tragic events. Some survivors with whom I have worked have engaged in deep breathing exercises and meditation in order to clear their minds of the distress they are experiencing. Others have used gardening or artistic activities to temporarily distract them from recurrent thoughts of their trauma until they are better able to handle their emotions. Still others have learned to use word exercises, either by writing in a journal or free writing, recording their words to connect images like flashbacks. This strategy helps the survivor to bring nonverbal images into articulated consciousness and reduces the anxiety attached to them. Other such calming and distracting approaches can be instrumental in allowing survivors to manage the post traumatic stress associated with the events they've experienced. Fortunately, there are many strategies that you, as a survivor, can utilize to this end. Be aware that these coping skills are most helpful when individualized, so find the one or ones which seem to aid you the most.

Many survivors over the years have sought my guidance to help them formulate a trauma recovery plan and take the first difficult steps on their individual healing journeys. In working with these survivors, I have incorporated and integrated various healing strategies. In many instances I try to be that "nudge," guiding them on the path through their early tentative beginnings. Typically, I begin by focusing on here-and-now strategies. These strategies include witnessing, reenactment, observation, reexperience and repair. I also utilize engaged conversation, attempting to establish an idea of what state the person is in physically, emotionally and spiritually. When you ventilate and retell your story to a sympathetic friend or counselor, you are validated in the process. Once feelings of safety and trust are established, many times survivors have been willing to allow me to bear witness to their trauma, both verbally and non-verbally. This allows for the reenactment and reexperience of their trauma from a controllable space. At this point, real physical and emotional repair can begin.

In order to reach the point of physical and emotional renewal, It is important to allow new insights and knowledge gained in the process of recovery into the present, in turn creating concrete positive changes in the here-and-now. It will be the most helpful if you make a conscious effort to organize your thoughts, feelings and behaviors. I therefore offer the survivors I work with the space for silent introspection. Many whom I have counseled have told me that the quietude gave them the space to confront and process their losses. For others, silent introspection allows them to submit to their losses and accept them as part of their lives' experiences. Stress-reduction skills training and education also promote recovery. When medication and other intervention seem needed, I strongly encourage professional counseling. Do not be afraid to seek this if you are stuck in the shock stage or grieving process and feel overwhelmed.

Though I utilize many different approaches and interventions, my client and I always move toward the same goal—healing. In general, however, the promotion of recovery entails emotional support. Emotional support can be verbal or non-verbal. I have never met a trauma survivor who has successfully recovered from his or her trauma solely through internal reflection. Having someone listen as you express your anguish goes a long way in promoting healing. Ultimately, for all survivors, the aim is to focus on strengths to develop new and healthier defenses and to foster self-empowerment.

However, this is not an easy task. Often survivors fiercely hold on to that which is already known even when such remedies are undertaken. Sometimes it takes a period of time to absorb what has happened before finding ways to move forward. For instance, Liz, a September 11th survivor, tried to interact with her family, friends, and coworkers as if "all was well" in the days after the attack. She went to church as she always had and listened quietly—hoping against hope that the service would be enough to comfort her. However, her old support system was not enough. As the days turned into weeks, the weeks turned into months and the months approached a year since her trauma, she still found little peace. The quality of her relationships was different also: she found herself able to interact only on a superficial level.

Liz also noticed that a good deal of the time she still felt very afraid. Her sleep continued to be interrupted throughout the night; she felt on edge and nervous with heart palpitations occurring daily.

"I don't feel like myself anymore," she told me.

I said, "I know you have spent your life caring for others, but in this time of traumatic stress, who is taking care of you? More importantly," I went on, "how can we get *you* to let others take care of you?"

She nodded. "My husband is constantly telling me that I'm always doing things for everyone else, trying to please everybody. I don't consider me most of the time."

I empathized with her. "I was there on September 11th too and I can't even imagine how bereft I would be without the support of family, friends and others. They've been instrumental in working through the experience of this tragedy. I have accepted my closest friend's love and support, her offer to sleep with the telephone next to her bed, urging me to call her at anytime if I need her. I have been grateful for my neighbor who, on many evenings, has knocked on my back door, holding a plate of food for a dinner I had been unable to make. I appreciate her husband, who became my chauffeur on occasion. 'You can make your professional telephone calls while I drive,' he had offered, so as to lessen, in this way, the many tasks I had to perform. Let others help you," I suggested.

She paused and then sighed, "I know you are right. I will try."

As time went on Liz and I also discussed applying a number of anxiety management strategies, self-care techniques and physical exercises to her daily schedule. At one later meeting, she decided that she would take daily walks and meditate on a regular basis to calm her body and soul. We also discussed ways in which she could allow her husband and children to help soothe her. "I need to get *me* back," she concluded. "A better me," she added.

Like Liz, another victim of trauma I worked with was Roger, who had witnessed a robbery in which his best friend was killed. He spoke of a state of generalized anxiety that inevitably was forestalling his healing process.

He said, "I feel awful. My legs feel weak and are trembling. I am having a hard time catching my breath and I am in a constant cold sweat. I continue to experience sharp pains in my stomach. At times, I feel like I am going to faint. One evening, my wife took me to the hospital. There I was told that I might have had a panic attack. Finally I decided I needed to stop working for a while.

Roger and I talked about utilizing physical exercise to work off stress and discussed whether a short-term trial of anti-anxiety medication might help to quell the constant jitters he had been feeling for many months. I referred Roger to a psychiatrist who would prescribe the right medication for him.

When I work with trauma survivors, my professional role revolves around diagnosing where they might need help as they begin their healing, providing education about the potential mental health effects of trauma at different periods in time and offering self-care strategies. I also provide referrals to psychotherapists, psychiatrists, support groups and other community resources. As healing and recovery begins, I regularly guide, support and monitor their progress as they begin to deal in more positive ways with the traumas they have suffered.

Coping with Trauma Repercussions

While many survivors slowly but steadily move forward and begin to recover, others continue to experience periods of great sadness, concentration difficulties, grief, intense anger and other normal responses to trauma. Survivors who have such problems have spoken to me of "triggers" that take them back emotionally to their traumatic events. Even as people begin to heal, they may at times be confronted with those symptoms that have persisted for months or, for some, years following their adversity. As I've indicated before, it is important for you who are survivors to understand that the recovery from trauma is not a linear path. Do not feel as though you are failing to progress. Like climbing steep hills, where you gain distance in increments along the way, there often are detours and backtracking before you reach the summit. On your way, you may approach another steep incline in the terrain of healing where acute symptoms may resurface. If this happens, pause to reassure yourself that this impediment to progress will pass. Recognize that other hills have been conquered already and that the current acute emotional state you are experiencing is another challenge but also an opportunity to learn. Such realizations and self reassurances are important tools in successfully negotiating one's healing path. Seeing the situation in this light, you will view the challenges you face along the way as incremental steps which may seem frustrating but will eventually lead to a positive journey.

Other problems which impede some survivors I have worked with are ongoing phobic and avoidance responses triggered by cues that resemble or symbolize aspects of their traumas. In such instances of acute re-traumatization, I provide repetitive crisis intervention sessions. For example, many months following the September 11th terrorist attacks, some survivors were still unable to take subways, board airplanes, ride elevators or enter high-rise buildings and continued to be fearful of loud noises and crowds. Those who had begun to force themselves to face these fears nonetheless continued to relate how fear still gripped them in such instances. Those who ventured into subways and elevators or tunnels spoke not only of anticipatory anxiety when entering into these situations but also of escalating anxiety when in such situations. Others remained persistently irritable and depressed. Still others experienced ongoing hyper-vigilance and sleep disturbances, including recurrent nightmares. Again, all of these experiences can occur if you have suffered trauma and most certainly do not signal that you will not recover, only that your recovery will take more time. Be patient with yourself.

For months following being accosted, threatened with death, robbed and severely beaten on a subway platform, Mara continued to exhibit phobic reactions and moderate depression. She was fearful of crowds and unable to enter subways or tunnels. She also experienced ongoing periods of tearfulness, felt isolated from family and friends and when a loud noise occurred stood near her front door in frozen panic. Eventually Mara realized she needed to get professional aid. She came to me for counseling and I sent her to see a psychiatrist who prescribed anti-depressant and anti-anxiety medications.

As her medication began to decrease her anxiety and our counseling sessions continued, she slowly started to do more and began interacting more with her family and friends. We talked about other small steps she could take to further help her progress on the her road to recovery: walking to the corner, progressing to walks around her block and then possibly walking her daughter to school at least once per week. Eventually, Mara began taking her daughter to school three days out of the week and was also able to leave her home for at least one hour per day. She admitted, however, that even though she was now leaving her home daily, if she went out one day she was more fearful of venturing out again the next. "I don't want to chance going out the next day, you know, push my luck," she related.

"Pushing her luck" was also closely tied to the yearly calendar and became a theme for many things in Mara's life. For example, the day and time of her trauma became significant triggers and she often re-experienced the event every month on that day. These markers often led her to put life on hold, not wanting to "push her luck."

Mara still had severe phobias to crowds, subways, tunnels and bridges. She experienced anticipatory anxiety connected to her phobias that escalated when placed in these situations. We talked through coping strategies and I went with her into the subway station without boarding the train. We used that experience to help her resolve the fear she felt until she felt able to cope with actually riding the train. We discussed taking a bus initially and using distracting and anxiety management techniques to deal with feelings of panic when entering tunnels or crossing bridges. As our time together went on, Mara practiced these coping strategies and while she continued to fear tunnels, subways and bridges, she regularly took the subway to work.

Another client, Therese, battled with a strong aversion to reminders of her trauma on 9/11. Nonetheless, she committed herself to the healing path and worked very hard to modify her tendency to avoidance. She followed through on the recommendation that she confront a real-life situation related to her trauma and to write down her emotional response afterwards.

As she recalls,"I decided I would 'see for myself' the office building we will be moving to in a couple of months. I've heard only negative things and wanted to judge for myself. A coworker and I walked over to the building. I was pleasantly surprised with the area. It was better than I had thought—rebuilt and refurbished.

"Next were the big steps: going into this twenty-plus story building, entering and showing ID to a guard who couldn't care less, as he made no attempt to check my ID. Then I had to take the elevator to an upper floor. I fought my panic after I got into this tiny elevator that couldn't fit more than four or five average-sized people. I realized that it was the first time I've been above the seventh floor of an office building since the event. I felt confined, hot and very nervous. I couldn't wait for the doors to open and then bring us right back down. I couldn't wait to get out of the building and outside into fresh air. I was very upset."

Therese took a painful but necessary step on the path to healing. While it was distressing to her, I pointed out that she had not been harmed and, in fact, showed great courage in even completing the task. I reminded her that each successive attempt she made to manage and cope with her fears and anxieties would lead to a greater sense of control and confidence.

I was positive that Therese was not totally convinced and when queried, Therese admitted that she continued to struggle to face, not avoid, triggers. I told her that admitting such an internal struggle existed was courageous. To acknowledge her struggle was a testament to the fact that she was beginning to cope rather than to deny, as she had done for many months. I empathized with her, reinforcing in her the need to move through the healing process at her own pace.

As our session continued she was able to realize that she needed to acknowledge and give herself credit for those steps she had taken so far, to be proud of her attempts to cope in the face of such tremendous fear. At intervals I asked Therese to recall all that she had done to cope thus far. Meanwhile, she continued to get up each morning, dress and go to work, confronting her fears of trains and elevators every day.

Some survivors I have counseled continue to be fearful of sounds that remind them of their traumas for a long time. They are easily startled by the slightest noise. Sheila, a young crime victim whom I counseled, expended much effort attempting to maintain her work performance in such an acutely traumatized state. When she entered my office, she showed a palpable sense of anxiety and restlessness. Her eyes darted around the office and she was extremely fidgety. I repeated my words to her slowly, as she was easily distracted and unable to maintain full concentration for any extended period of time. When I articulated my observations of her ongoing anxiety, we devised a self-care plan in which she agreed to spend her time when not in the office engaging in relaxing and soothing activities. We also talked about decreasing her sugar intake and making attempts to read entertaining novels as a way of increasing her concentration level.

Other survivors whom I've counseled have experienced persistent feelings of irritability and anger after their traumas. Over time, some sufferers directed unresolved angry feelings toward their family, friends and peers.

Steff, a September 11th survivor, came to me not only with angry feelings toward his boss, but also for his family and friends. While his explanations for his anger seemed plausible on the surface, I wondered whether his anger was excessive and misplaced. As we talked further, Steff began to express tremendous sadness about the death of one of his colleagues. As we talked more and more, it seemed that his irritability and anger were manifestations of this trauma and its common reverberating effects. Steff also admitted that since this trauma, he felt his own subjective shortcomings and saw that he might be contributing to the perceived negativity around him. He confided that he saw himself as "being at a fork in the road" and felt compelled to make hard decisions regarding his occupational, interpersonal and inner life. He questioned the manner in which he presently negotiated his work relationships, social networks and family interactions. With further exploration, it became clear that Steff needed to formulate a better, more positive sense of himself. As he began to express his grief and, at the same time, enhance, build and make more solid those relationships that were important to him, his persistent irritability and anger melted away.

Singular Vistas

Although there are numerous common reactions to trauma that may persist over time, some may experience one lasting symptom while others may experience many simultaneously. Remember, there are many ways to reach the same healing place. This is also true when dealing with recurrent distress reactions. For instance, those dealing with childhood sexual abuse often need empowerment in such areas as personal boundaries and self-esteem. Survivors of a loved one's murder may need to address issues of misplaced blame and responsibility.

For any survivor of a traumatic event there needs to be an unlocking of the self-protection mode and its defensive underpinnings, because these mechanisms inhibit people who have been traumatized from moving beyond the experience. Although self-protection is required in the midst of trauma, this mode sometimes remains automatic long after it is no longer needed. To mend, survivors must move beyond extreme self-protection in order to lessen their tension and anxiety.

Various Paths to Healing

It is helpful, in general, for survivors to receive relaxation training, training in assertiveness and stress management techniques as well as couple and family counseling. Learning techniques to help soothe the self and utilize problem-solving skills and coping mechanisms are also beneficial. In addition, while some fare best on medication, cognitive behavioral treatments that aim to teach healthy behaviors and restructure thinking to achieve a more balanced perspective, as well as guided imagery, exposure and group therapies, will aid in facilitating recovery for a large percentage of survivors.

I have found several techniques to be of particular support to those suffering from trauma's aftermath. Eye Movement Desensitization and Reprocessing (EMDR) sessions are structured to allow survivors to re-live their cataclysmic experience through each of the senses so that the event is laid out in all its manifestations and dimensions. This approach is viewed by some mental health professionals as important for the full processing of traumatic events. There are many accounts of survivors who, years later, suddenly found themselves retraumatized by sounds, images or thoughts that had been encoded in their brains at the time of their traumas yet never brought to consciousness. EMDR techniques seemed to not only bring her experience forward for Therese, it helped her reprocess the experience from a "controllable" view, a vantage point utterly lacking in the initial event. In this way, integration and healing truly began for her.

I have found that still other survivors reconnect with their spirituality through active participation in prayer or rituals. For those with persistent generalized fear and situation-specific anxieties, deep breathing exercises and positive self-talk may work. For example, they may repeat, "I have lived safely for the past thirty years and there was only one time when it was problematic. The odds are in my favor." Some survivors feel more comfortable facing their fears by talking them out with friends and loved ones until the fear response becomes less paralyzing. Others are helped when they carry recreational items like tape players, video games or books with them on stress-inducing outings.

Overall, it is important that survivors manage life in a manner in keeping with their individual value systems. It is also necessary for survivors to direct their own recoveries, gather relevant information and seek support from various sources. Ultimately, in order to regain a measure of control over their own lives, all survivors need to choose whether or not to accept feedback. To accept feedback allows them to seek help yet doesn't obligate them to accept unwanted help. It is critical that survivors believe in their own abilities to recover. At the same time, communication revolving around acknowledging feelings without the need to apologize for uncertainty or justify feelings to others can lead to a greater sense of empowerment. The acknowledgment of feelings while working on processing trauma's repercussions denies the traumatic event the ability to impact the survivor's quality of life. At the point in their journeys when they can freely express their feelings, I have heard many survivors begin to give reasons for resuming active living as opposed to existing in states of fear and grief. Be reassured you too can reach this point.

The Role of Integration in the Healing Process

Containing, rather than controlling, feelings is another important step in integrating the trauma you have suffered and a key to reorganizing your life. Reaching the point of this undertaking involves transforming painful states of being into personal narratives that are then integrated into your expanded self. Accepting and integrating all domains of one's trauma without the intensity of adverse affects concludes this process.

I start my counseling process by assessing where each person is in the restorative process and then try to guide the person in developing personalized approaches that will work for that person. In our dialogues and encounters, I try to enhance resilience and facilitate the view of change as challenge rather than threat. When a survivor addresses all the dimensions of trauma in a safe environment, the whole person, emotions, body, mind and spirit begin to heal. As a survivor, view this process as an ongoing one. Such a psychological outlook will allow you to see yourself as a healthy individual in a continuous state of development and self-growth, despite the trauma you have experienced.

Reconnecting with the Self

In my own journey to healing after September 11th, I questioned at one stage whether I was taking care of myself. In addition to my private practice patients, I was meeting with an average of twelve World Trade Center survivors a day. I also continued to maintain ongoing sessions with my mentor. As I constantly straddled the line between helper and survivor, an insidious emotional toll began to be exacted. I noticed that the line between helper and trauma survivor was becoming blurred and difficult to maintain. I started to avoid interactions with my own family and friends. Once home each evening, all I desired was sleep, to get away from the pain and suffering I felt and was encountering on a daily basis. Perhaps you too have also experienced similar feelings of distress for a period of time or are still at this difficult juncture. Let my own experiences aid in helping you recognize that you should not feel guilty when you need some self-care strategies, as I did, to bolster resilience in order to handle post traumatic stress. In my case, I knew that my ability to help survivors would be greatly undermined if I did not address these problems. In fact, your ability to help the others in your life will be impeded if you do not relieve your own turmoil.

Once I realized this I began by exercising after work each evening, doing basic stretching and deep muscle relaxation. I awoke one morning during this period with the thought that repainting my apartment would be a fun and therapeutic task. I lay in bed for several minutes and envisioned each room as a potentially creative process, serving both a functional and an aesthetic purpose. In my mind, I chose gentle colors and plush carpeting. I went to a paint store that day. That evening I began my project. Perhaps you too can regain contentment by sprucing up your surroundings.

At this point in my own journey, I also refocused on my personal relationships, reconnecting with friends and family, planning dinners and theatre, and setting up "catch up" dates at local cafés. I made plans to get away for long weekends and on several occasions I took along a friend or family member to my Cape Cod home. At other times, I made the five-hour trek to Cape Cod alone, for, at this point in my healing journey, solitude and peace no longer felt like avoidance and isolation. I had rediscovered my zone of emotional health and was beginning to feel rejuvenated. I also addressed the symptoms and causes of my stress with my mentor. In fact, as time went on, work with my mentor led to personal enrichment and the incentive to enhance my clinical skills. As I regained the necessary balance between my professional and personal life, I could continue to help other survivors regain their equilibrium. You too need to give yourself permission to take the time and find ways to regain your own sense of balance.

Through the advice in this book, hopefully you will reach the point where you can refocus and reformulate a rewarding life despite the trauma you have experienced.

Chapter 7 Resilience Tips

- Write down all you have learned about how your trauma uniquely manifests itself in you.
- Recognize that the stages of trauma do not flow in a straight line and that you have probably improved even if you are still experiencing difficult symptoms.
- List the feelings, behaviors, thoughts and physiological reactions that have faded or subsided since the event.
- List the approaches you believe helped those reactions to fade or subside.
- Determine if any of your successful strategies can be directly applied or modified to reduce any current distressing reactions.
- Consider whether your ongoing distress may be caused by a "blockage" or is the result of being stuck in a particular stage of recovery. For example, if you are persistently angry, you may be stuck in the anger stage of grief. If you are stuck, think about what you can do that will be helpful in moving you toward the next stage of your healing. Follow through on your options.
- Assess where you are and what you feel at this point.
- Use relaxation techniques and reaching out to friends and family to enrich and refocus.
- Make an honest determination as to whether you can work through the particular aspect of grief, anxiety or pain you now are experiencing or whether you may most benefit from professional counseling. Remember, you may need assistance to help you to move through a particularly difficult stage of reaction to your trauma. Your goal is recovery and healing.

EXERCISE

List the core beliefs that you identified in the chapter 5 exercise section below. Then, next to each belief, rewrite your belief in a way that incorporates your traumatic experience in a more balanced way.

For example,

CORE BELIEF
Bad things should not happen to good people

INTEGRATED BELIEF
While adverse events happen to good people, good people can overcome them and are more likely to have other good people around for help and support.

CORE BELIEF

INTEGRATED BELIEF

_____   _____

_____   _____

_____   _____

_____   _____

_____   _____

_____   _____

_____   _____

_____   _____

_____   _____

Chapter 8

A New Normal:
Evolving Horizons

As we have seen, post-trauma existence for many survivors is weighty and burdensome. Many survivors seek to relieve their burdens by displacing their traumas using a variety of distractions. Some, like meditation, are positive; some, like alcohol abuse, are negative. It can be comforting for you who are suffering to realize that though each survivor progresses at a different rate and may take a different route, recovery can and does take place. When survivors reach the crossroads at which they can acknowledge that their traumas are real, the need to incorporate their ordeals into their internal and external lives becomes an imperative goal. This goal signifies yet another shift in self and worldview and often leads to positive lifelong changes. And when there are such changes within the self, it begins to blossom, enhancing the individual's outward reality. At this point survivors accept having lived through chaos and loss and develop a "new normal."

Gaining New Insights

Intertwined with personality traits, prior coping skills and the other personal attributes that make each one of us unique, every survivor's new normal is being self-defined through a process of forming new personal insights into who they were, who they could become and what they truly need, want and desire. While each arrival at this stage of a new normal has been a painful personal journey, the outcomes for many are extraordinary.

Among those whose evolution I have witnessed, Brandon treaded through the aftermath of his trauma virtually repeating the mantra, "It's not about the job." Initially unable to reconcile his mantra with his pre-trauma self, Brandon was consumed with fear, self-doubt and an acute sense of isolation. He seemed to constantly ask himself, *If it is not about the job, then what is it about? What then is my norm?* During the many months in which he labored to come to terms with his past trauma, Brandon also found himself learning who he really was and what he most desired in life. "It's about my family," he stated, nearly a year after his traumatic event. "It's about me in relation to my family," he concluded.

Essentially, Brandon found his new normal and began to act on his self-discoveries. He prioritized that which was ultimately of greatest importance to him—his wife, children, relatives, friends and his quality of life. As he explained, "The trauma I suffered woke me up and showed me what was truly important to me personally and professionally. I did not want to leave my job out of fear. But, I had to conclude that my career choice was largely based on financial security and not a true love for the job. I now want to live a more fulfilling and satisfying life and be there for my wife and children."

Brandon said that when he reached his awakening, he felt as if a weight had been lifted from his shoulders. This lifting of his burden was closely followed by a scene of peace he had failed to enjoy since his ordeal. His new and expanded "normal" opened a new chapter in his life.

After close to two-and-one-half years in treatment, Carol integrated her trauma and took back her life. She chipped away at the self-sabotaging behaviors that, while seeming to defend her against emotional pain, were keeping her locked away from opportunities of self-discovery and love. Her new normal began as she let go of self-fulfilling prophecies of failure and the persistent acts through which she pushed others out of her life. Carol started to allow others to show who they were as individuals instead of assuming that everyone around her was poised to hurt her emotionally. In due course, Carol got to know herself not as someone who had been permanently and irrevocably damaged by her ordeal but as a person who was "becoming." Carol said, "In my mind, my trauma was indeed horrific and for decades I accepted blame and believed that I somehow caused it. But in making sense of it all from a more realistic perspective, I now fully believe that I was no more responsible for my trauma than I was for my birth. But while I am here on this earth I will take responsibility for my life. The pain of my trauma no longer defines me."

Carol eloquently noted that the chipping away of her damaged self-identity was analogous to tearing down a brick wall and allowing rays of light to pour through. Afterward, she lived a new normal—a normal that encompassed disappointment and encouragement, pain and love, sadness and joy. Embarking on her new path, Carol traveled with hope and positive plans for the future. With this new outlook, Carol began to make positive changes in her life including entering graduate school to earn an advanced degree.

Integration and the Expanded Self

As Alyce integrated the trauma she'd experienced into her life, she reconnected with her spirituality. She went on weekend spiritual retreats and read books on spirituality. One philosophy resonated with her in particular; it focused on reclaiming self-love through connections with family and friends. As she noted, "My trauma helped me realize that life should be lived to the fullest and that it is precious. I started to appreciate my family and friends more." As Alyce forged stronger bonds with those close to her, she began to act as if she had a future. She started talking about a five-year plan of personal and professional goals. She began promoting her catering business.

After Steff integrated his ordeal he began to recruit Christian singers and produced an album. As he worked on this project his manner was relatively easy and relaxed. He seemed to exude a confidence that enlarged as he finally settled into his "new normal." Steff related, "I was able to make sense of the events and all that followed by way of my religious beliefs. I saw the event as a wake up call for me to stop procrastinating and become more determined to fulfill God's purpose for me in this life—the gift of producing Christian music."

Although Bob never fully recovered from the physical injuries he'd sustained in the trauma he'd suffered, he nonetheless became happier and more at peace. He rediscovered his humorous side, a side of himself that he had tucked away when still in his early twenties. He told me that his wife and son now seem to look upon him approvingly and with fresh, loving eyes, because he is able to laugh again. He has also enthusiastically followed through on his passion for trains by working with his son to build model trains. Bob shared with me, "For me, the realization that even though tragedies do happen to good people, adversity can be like a magic wand in expanding an individual's horizons." Bob successfully integrated different parts of himself—the father, businessman, husband and jokester—but he did not lose his natural complexity and inner richness. He now emanated self-assurance without arrogance. He was generous to others without expecting anything in return.

Like Bob, at the point of her integration, Janet, whose father was murdered, also was able to give freely of herself. Receiving positive emotions, she was able to give them back ten-fold. "It's amazing," she remarked. "The more I give, the more I get. It took me years to make sense of it all and during that time I was filled with self-doubt. Part of that had to do with my age when the murder occurred. But then I realized in amazement how one person, in ten short years, could instill such positive and wonderful traits in another human being and the potential effects on anyone who comes into contact with that positive energy. "

Janet added, "Six degrees of separation says it all. If I can pass on those things I learned from my father to people I come in contact with on a daily basis, his positive human legacy will live on and on."

In making these connections, Janet finally integrated her trauma and in the process rediscovered herself, the self that for so long was locked inside her grief. At the same time, she also began to appreciate others for whom they were and not in comparison to her father—a tendency she was able to acknowledge only after accepting the reality of her father's death and after gaining the ability to appreciate the times they had shared together.

Each of these survivors reached the point of integration in his or her own way. I hope you will gain revived hope that you can find the best path for yourself, as they did, if you keep searching.

As Mara said, "I made sense of the event through prayer and therapy. I also began to believe that my contribution to this world is to give back, to help people more. So, I try now to be even more helpful to others." Always a helper Mara ultimately saw her trauma as reinforcing these traits. However, I also encouraged Mara, in addition to helping others, to be helpful to herself through continued self-care that would fortify her physically, spiritually and emotionally.

Therese reported that when she began to reach integration it was obvious to her due to the fact that she experienced less tearful and anxious days and "more and more calm ones." In an attempt to further integrate her trauma, Therese began to write down her story, a task she admitted was extremely difficult to even contemplate when she was in the grasp of her suffering. Although she had to stop writing several times, she eventually completed her narrative. As Therese surmised, "In reevaluating my beliefs, I became more aware of people. I don't ever want to be helpless as I felt that day and I want others to know that though they may feel grief stricken afterward, they can eventually heal and recover as I did." Therese, an example of successful recovery, strengthened her assets, took decisive action toward healing, accepted her limitations and nurtured helping relationships.

Still other survivors have shared with me varied ways integration and renewal occurred for them. Said Corki, "When I could look back with self-realization and insight, I realized the event made me stronger and helped me put things in perspective. I know that I am blessed. I don't get caught up in petty things anymore."

As she healed, Corki saw the event as an opportunity to lessen the strain of continually concerning herself with what others might think of her. She began to accept herself. She came to recognize that as a person she was born with certain rights: the right to ask for what she wanted, the right to feel scared, the right to have her needs and wants respected by others and the right to change and grow.

Corki put her always-please-others internal voice to rest and in the process learned to take better care of herself. Her new normal encompassed not only self-care, but also the ability to engage in pleasurable and relaxing activities. This new focus allowed her the energy to give freely and lovingly to her family and friends. In essence, Corki's new normal provided her with a stronger self-identity while strengthening her bonds with those close to her.

For Antoinette, integration first manifested itself through her physical body. At each successive visit, she grew visibly stiller and less jittery. The stress lines on her face slowly diminished and a glimmer of brightness entered her eyes. During this period she also began going to the gymnasium and signed up for classes at a local college. At one of our recent meetings, she stated proudly, "I'm controlling what is controllable." She also noted, "Listening to non-mainstream radio and reading different newspapers helped me make sense of it all. These forums gave me a different perspective and helped me gain more knowledge about the world around me. I also stopped procrastinating and started taking care of personal business. I stopped putting off things. The event showed me that I could no longer take for granted that I can wait to do things."

As her new normal took hold, Antoinette's ability to find inner strength, to be decisive and to follow through on decisions surfaced. It was as if the anxiety that plagued her body in the aftermath of her trauma became channeled into purposeful behavior that, in the end, enriched her life. Equally important to her internalized new normal was her drive toward an expanded worldview, which, in turn, unlocked many other possibilities for her.

Liz shared with me the insight that integrating her trauma changed how she moved in her environment and in her world. "I used to get caught up in the craziness and now I'm deciding what is best for me. For the first time in my life, I'm taking care of me first," she said. I asked her to verbalize this process.

"For one, I practice deep breathing and positive self-thinking to help me remain calm," she said.

"What do you say to yourself that's positive?" I asked.

"I tell myself, 'Liz, do one thing at a time. It's okay to take your time.'"

"Anything else?" I asked.

"I also allow myself breaks, something I would have never done before. These breaks give me a chance to reenergize myself. I don't have to please everybody every time," she replied. "I also try to keep negative energy at bay."

"How?" I asked.

"I tell myself, 'I don't have to go there with this person' or 'I don't have to get caught up in the negativity.'"

As she shared with me numerous other ways in which she

had integrated her experience and, in due course, had reached higher personal heights in a "new normal," I applauded her. I verbally acknowledged how far she had come and what great courage she had demonstrated, emphasizing that to rethink how she moved about in her world and to lay claim to a new normal was a daunting task. I shared with her my conclusion that her ability to act in this new world in a positive and healthy manner demonstrated her strength and resilience. I reminded her that some people, metaphorically, never get beyond acting as if they were in their old, comfortable shoes. This is not because they are weak people, but simply because these shoes are indeed comfortable. They are not always ideal for a given challenge or for healing and recovery, though. I reminded her of the strides she had made and I encouraged her to forge ahead and step confidently, as I knew she could, further along the path to healing.

Yet there was another challenge ahead for Liz—returning to the area where her trauma occurred. In order to help her do this, one morning Liz and I sat down and began the process of desensitizing her. Our goal was to help her manage her fears, both the anticipatory anxiety and the anxiety that would be triggered upon her return to the area of trauma. We listed each step of the process—from waking up in the morning and knowing she had to go to the area to actually being there and working in the area. We rated the anxiety level connected to each step on a scale of 0 – 100, with 100 being the most anxious she could possibly imagine.

Liz's List

1.	Waking up at home	0
2.	Waking up and knowing she would be going to the area where her trauma occurred	30
3.	Getting dressed	30
4.	Getting into her car and driving to the subway	40
5.	Walking down the steps leading to the subway	50
6.	Paying the subway fare and going through the turnstile	60
7.	Walking to the subway platform	70
8.	Getting on the train	80

9.	Feeling the rumbling of the train as it traveled through the tunnel	90
10.	Feeling the train stopping in the dark tunnel between stations	90
11.	Exiting the train	90
12.	Climbing the steps to the street level	90
13.	Standing on a city street corner	100
14.	Walking into her new office building	100
15.	Getting on the elevator to go to her office	100

We discussed which anxiety management and coping strategies she could effectively use for each step. We decided that for anxiety levels ranging between 10 and 30, Liz would use deep breathing exercises. For anxiety levels between 31 and 50, she would use distracting techniques like counting change in her pocket, positive self-talk and other coping statements. Liz decided that she would use all available techniques for anxiety levels between 50 and 70 and would use thought-stopping techniques for anxiety levels greater than seventy.

We selected a day on which I would accompany her on her first trip into the area. I recommended that we plan on getting to the subway station and then decide if we would exit the train or return immediately.

As expected, the first trip back to the trauma area was anxiety-provoking for Liz. She experienced sweaty palms and heart palpitations after boarding the subway car and as the train rumbled through the tunnel. Deep breathing and positive self-talk got her through these tough steps. When the train stopped in the tunnel between stations, I told Liz that she was doing beautifully and asked her what would be helpful to her in that moment. She decided to read affirmations and she practiced thought-stopping techniques. We reached our destination.

We decided to go to the street level. Liz's knees buckled slightly as we made our way up the stairs. I held her arm reassuringly. She stopped briefly, took a deep breath and we then exited to the street level. Silently, we stood together for several minutes as Liz looked about. Finally, Liz said, with amazement in her voice, "Everything is the same. People are walking around. The same buildings are here. The same stores are here. And I'm here. This is not bad!"

We made the same trip together on several additional occasions. Each trip took us closer to her place of employment and, in due course, Liz began working in the area again with minimal anxiety and fear.

Learning Resilience

For many of these survivors, their new normal is contingent on enhancing resilience or the ability to adapt to difficult and challenging experiences. As they travel along their healing paths to reach their new normals, survivors learn resilience and living techniques including coping skills, the acceptance of change, gaining a long-term perspective and nurturing of each self. For most survivors, learning personal resilience goes hand in hand with garnering the support and help of others they trusted and who provided reassurance and encouragement. After some time and self-searching, sometimes paired with professional counseling, I have found that survivors become their own experts on how best to heal.

As the survivors I have known and counseled learned resilience and adjusted to their new normals, an assortment of personal attributes began to emerge. Some began to exhibit improved self-confidence, greater trust in their decision-making and the ability to cope more effectively with the emotions connected to their ordeals. Some began to recognize previously hidden talents while others demonstrated stronger self-esteem. Still others gained improved skills in managing distressing emotions or showed renewed focus on self-development and growth, which led to higher levels of purpose and fulfillment. Overall, in countless ways, treasures inherent in each survivor appeared to become available to the person and then each one moved forward to a future enhanced by all he or she now knows and has become.

I have felt honored to bear witness to these survivors' transformations. I have been humbled by the tenacity of survivors in their pursuit of such transformations. I know how each of these individuals suffered, struggled and faltered on their healing paths. I also know the strength it took for each survivor to forge ahead despite the immense pain of trauma, grief and loss. I have watched this courage as it became unbounded by self-limitation. Beholding life's richness through the eyes of these people, I too have been transformed.

Because of their examples, I have felt better equipped to sustain both my professional and personal self in the face of my own trials. I have learned to understand more deeply the possibility of failure as well as the potential for fulfillment after one has suffered a traumatic event. Now I believe in the worthiness of my own life's work on a level higher than ever before.

I have personally experienced the effects of trauma as I processed it and as it tested my knowledge, skills and the techniques I used to combat it, on my worst critic—myself. As time has passed and I have moved forward on my path, I have noticed how the anxieties and fears precipitated by my own trauma have finally settled down. In their place resolve has emerged. I have gained new insights into myself and embarked on a self-journey that includes taking healthy risks and living life unconditionally. I have also realized parts of myself that may never have been revealed had it not been for the traumatic experience I went through. I have successfully tackled intense periods of fear and, in time, reached higher levels of resilience. You who suffer as I did will, I hope, take comfort in my steps along my journey, a healing path on which I have confidence you also can embark.

Expanding Horizons

Like me, you as a survivor will be able to live in an expanded reality that is integrated with, not separated from, your individual traumatic experience. You can embrace your new normal and find hidden treasures in life. As you reach this pinnacle you will be able to make time for what's really important and this will, I believe, become a recurrent affirmation as you move along your individual healing path and learn to live again.

Some of you will find extra comfort in being part of a support group and developing bonds with other survivors. Still others will find renewed attachment and connection with their own self-defined senses of spirituality.

Some of you will become more focused on the world around you and reflect on how you related to the world before your trauma and how you related after your ordeal. If you are one of these survivors, you consequently will express a need to be more proactive in making the world a better place through such acts as volunteerism and community activism. Like still other survivors, you may find renewed appreciation for your immediate and extended families. You may begin embarking on goals that you had put off for years. Still others of you will reintroduce yourselves to hobbies and other pleasures for which you previously felt you had no time. Whatever the trauma, with each step along your individual healing path, you who are the survivors will grow stronger, more resilient and better defined as individuals. And your unique horizons will continue to evolve infinitely. Trust me, I know all this is true, for I have walked the difficult but healing path to recovery.

Chapter 8 Resilience Tips

- Finally accepting the full reality of our trauma, we also open ourselves to a new normal.
- Think about ways in which you have come to terms with your loss(es).
- List the behaviors, thoughts and feelings that you believe have previously impeded your ability to heal and cope effectively with your trauma.
- List the activities, thought processes, advice, etcetera that helped you on your journey.
- List some of the positive ways you think, feel and act.
- Write down what you have learned about yourself in these areas:
    1. The ability to adapt to difficult situations
    2. Inner strength
    3. Resilience
- What long-term goals or plans did you have prior to your ordeal?
- What ideas and thoughts have you explored since reaching integration of your trauma?
- What new goals or plans are you now making?

Chapter 9

Trauma Reactions
and Healing Paths
for Children and Adolescents

While children and adolescents who experience traumatic events have trauma reactions similar to those felt by adults, such as fear, depression and anxiety, the individual's stage of development plays a significant role in how each child exhibits distress and, in turn, how traumatic events may impact his or her maturation.

When children suffer their own or loved ones traumas they look toward the family system to "right" that which is now terribly wrong. If the family system is also overwhelmed, a child may feel abandoned and shift into a self-protection mode in an attempt at self-preservation. Yet, because of their young ages and limited cognitive, behavioral, emotional and coping skills, children often are unable to successfully negotiate such upheavals without help from adults or professionals in their lives in both understanding and handling traumas. This is especially true if they exhibit behavior characteristic of post-traumatic stress.A traumatized three- or four-year-old, for instance, may show signs of regression to a pre-toilet training or baby-talk period, possibly necessitating retraining in these areas. Retraining him or her delays the child's entry into the next developmental stage typical for that child's age.

We live in an increasingly violent society and the likelihood of children being exposed to traumatic events is higher than ever before. Events leading to traumatic responses in children range in character from witnessing violent crime, suffering incest or sexual abuse to larger scale damages caused by such events as terrorism, war, hostage-taking or natural disasters. These and other traumatic events can cause children and adolescents to feel depression and anxiety.

Post-traumatic reactions may show immediately following traumatic events or weeks or months later. Reactions such as flashbacks, withdrawal behavior, loss of trust in adults, fears of going outside or planes overhead, sleep disturbances, fear of the event occurring again and traumatic play, (for instance, the child re-enacts the event through drawings or assumes the role of a major aspect or victim of the event). When experienced by children, traumatic events can lead to a diverse range of responses, many of which are experienced by adults. Yet, unlike adults, children are often likely to exhibit traumatic distress through behavior.

Preschool Children: Ages One through Five

In large measure, preschool children attempt to deal with traumatic events through behavior. Often, preschool children engage in play during which they reenact distressing aspects of the trauma. This play may take the form of obsessively acting out elements of the trauma. Four-year-old Jennifer, a child who had witnessed a violent crime, used a rolled up sheet of paper to simulate a gun. Peter, another young witness, repeatedly ran through his home "stabbing" family members and visitors after witnessing the stabbing of a stranger while in a mall with his parents. It should also be noted that traumatic play is often interspersed with normal play.

Some preschoolers who have been witnesses or victims engage in regressive behaviors such as thumb-sucking, fear of darkness, whimpering and bed-wetting. Others develop physical responses such as unexplained stomach aches, loss of appetite and generalized aches and pains. Preschoolers also may become terrified of strangers and express their anxiety through irritable or angry behavior. Some may even resort to self-injurious behavior, including hair-pulling, scratching themselves with their fingernails or head-banging.

Grammar School Children: Ages Six through Eleven

Regressive behavior may also occur in elementary school-age children. This may take the form of separation anxiety from caretakers and generally clingy behavior. Children exposed to trauma in this age group may become more aggressive and exhibit oppositional behavior toward others. Like adults, children six to eleven may develop hypervigilence, difficulties in paying attention, irrational fears and avoidant behavior or at the other extreme, they may become avid risk-takers, provoking older and stronger children, displaying aggression and engaging in dangerous behavior.

Pre-adolescent and Adolescents: Ages Twelve through Seventeen

In this age group, there is a high risk of suicidal behavior (with the oldest young people being at highest risk). Suicide is one of the leading causes of death in adolescents. Therefore, symptoms of depression, alcohol or substance abuse, high-risk or self-injurious behavior should be vigilantly assessed and acted on immediately, either through psychiatric evaluation and/or hospitalization.

While as a whole this age group is more cognitively developed, they can also exhibit regressive behavior in the aftermath of traumatic events. Some teens and preteens suddenly become more "homebound" and engage less in age-appropriate peer relationships. Others avoid school, become dependent, socially withdrawn or anxious. On the other hand, some teenagers run away or become more antisocial by stealing, vandalizing, using drugs and alcohol or by being sexually promiscuous. Risk-taking and distinctive changes in grooming or dressing habits (such as wearing all black or heavy makeup) may also occur in this age group. Some pre-teens and teens also become more defiant in their homes and aggressively provocative toward authority figures.

Deterioration in their school performance following a traumatic event is more common in this age group than in the six to eleven age group. The latter group may actually show improved school performance following traumatic events, as school may offer these children a structure that diminishes disturbing feelings about the world being chaotic. Pre-teens and teens may also complain of having chronic aches and pains, exhibit sleep disturbances and develop skin conditions.

Overall, child and adolescent trauma survivors exhibit responses unique to their age and developmental stage at the time of the events. Therefore, when a child or adolescent is traumatized, it is important for adults to keep in mind that any changes in behavior (including withdrawal behavior) is likely to reflect the child's response to the event. A change in behavior is often a child's attempt to communicate his or her distress. It is important that caretakers take steps to alleviate such distress in children as long term effects may worsen.

Lauren, eight years old, was a trauma victim. Lauren and her mother were clothes shopping for the upcoming school year. As they stepped off the curb and into the street, they heard a screeching sound closely followed by a bumping noise. Instinctively, both Lauren and her mother stepped back on the sidewalk. Then they looked in the direction of the noise and saw the bleeding body of a teenage boy lying in the street across from where they stood.

Initially, according to her mother, Lauren's body became as still as a mannequin. Then, she began to shake uncontrollably, clenching her mother's hand so tightly it caused bruising. As people around them raced to the aid of the teenager, Lauren and her mother, both in shock, were unable to move. Eventually, Lauren's mother turned them away from the scene. Lauren, however, felt compelled to look back at the scene of the accident as they walked away. Lauren later recalled that she never saw the teenager move again and that the ambulance workers seemed unhurried in their responses to get him to a hospital.

At home that evening, Lauren's mother noticed that Lauren did not eat her dinner and complained of having a stomachache. Recognizing that Lauren's lack of appetite was likely due to the event, Lauren's mother allowed her to go upstairs to her bedroom. Later she talked with her daughter about the event. Lauren told her mother that she believed the teenager had died and she wondered out loud how his family might be feeling.

Over the next several weeks, Lauren behaved more and more uncharacteristically. Instead of begging her mother to let her spend time with her best friend or to take her to the shopping mall as she often had in the past, Lauren now seemed constantly "underfoot," and looked panic-stricken when her mother was not in sight. Lauren also continued to experience poor appetite and told her mother that she was having "scary dreams" but was unable to describe them. Lauren only said that she "just woke up scared in the middle of the night." Later, Lauren began coming into her mother's room and getting in bed with her.

According to her mother, Lauren became easily startled and was often "jittery." Her mother also noted that these behaviors were particularly acute when they were out of the house. Lauren also tried to avoid being in cars, buses or trains and reported feeling nonspecific aches and pains whenever there were family plans to travel outside.

Finally, Lauren's mother called me and mad an appointment. When I first saw her, Lauren had regressed to an earlier developmental stage and our task was to help her work through the trauma she had witnessed and move her toward her true developmental stage and independence. Her traumatic experience also resulted in hypervigilence and avoidance behavior that would require attention in order to "normalize" her life and overall development. Thankfully, Lauren was old enough to differentiate between intentional and accidental acts. Therefore I felt working through the trauma could take place from a more cognitive frame of reference than with a younger child. Nonetheless, the process of cognitive growth was still under way and therefore play therapy also had an important role. It was during such play therapy that Lauren revealed that after seeing the accident she had a constant worry about dying. Once she had verbalized this feeling, we were able to discuss it and this worry dissipated.

Over the course of treatment Lauren and I worked on anxiety-reducing skills to address her hypervigilence, which resulted from the unexpected and sudden nature of the accident she witnessed. Attention was also paid to issues of safety as they pertained to her stage of development. Since we wanted her to move toward peer development and independence, we addressed how she might begin to feel a sense of safety that would help her to regain the appropriate stage of development and continue to mature. I helped her to become more comfortable and willing to interact with her peers rather than clinging to her mother.

Using interactive games and artistic mediums such as drawing and verbal exchanges, I reflected back to Lauren the themes that were present in her play. These included issues of safety, fear, anxiety and regressive behavior. During such reenactments, I provided general information and taught her skills of mastery. One such mastery skill involved Lauren "taking" her mother out on an errand. In this situation, Lauren was "in charge" of picking the day, time and the items for which she and her mother shopped. Eventually, over time, friends and school activities began to take on more and more importance in Lauren's life and she was able to function in a well-adjusted, happy manner.

Anthony was another childhood trauma victim. An avid base-ball player and ninth-grade honors student, he lost his seventeen-year-old brother in an automobile accident. Anthony's parents even-tually brought their seven-year-old daughter to me because she was exhibiting regressive behavior, including a heretofore unseen fear of being left in the dark. When I asked how Anthony, her older brother was doing, his parents stated that Anthony was "handling everything pretty well," pointing to his continuing excellent grades in school and his newly found "over-protectiveness toward his baby sister." However, as my questions continued, Anthony's parents realized that their son was overprotective of them as well. They noted that he recently began "acting like a little man," and had become less involved with his friends and baseball. When I pointed out that Anthony's behavior might also indicate depression, his parents agreed that all members of the household should meet together to help the family work through their tragedy. During our first session, Anthony admitted that a part of him "felt old." So, an equally impor-tant goal became helping both children regain their footing and return to behaving in age-appropriate ways. Other treatment goals were to help the family members renegotiate their roles and responsibilities. To do so, it is important to work on developing new skills necessary to manage the current tragedy and future life-altering events.

Helping Children and Families Reconnect

When tragedy strikes a family, parents or other caretakers and family members need to pay very close attention to the children, while work-ing to return to the family's normal routine as quickly as possible. It is always helpful to talk with each child about what happened and to give them plenty of reassurance. Let children know that feeling upset is normal and allow them to be sad or cry. It should also be noted that, depending on the developmental stage of the child at the time of the trauma, talking about the trauma may occur over weeks, months and even years. For example, a child who lost a parent at age five will have more sophisticated concerns and questions about the parent's death at age thirteen.

After therapy, Lauren and Anthony were able to pick up where they left off developmentally. They both developed coping and prob-lem-solving skills to help reduce avoidance behavior and catastrophiz-ing (so they would not magnify negative elements of events to such an extent that they were represented as disasters from which there can be no recovery) as well as finding methods for managing their anxiety. In both cases, the ultimate goal was to help their family systems function to support each member and to work together to manage their ordeals. In Lauren's case, I also worked with her mother to help her address Lauren's trauma. Her mother's support was instrumental in Lauren's recovery. I also worked with Lauren's mother to help her manage her own responses to the event. Similarly, Anthony would have had an extremely difficult time returning to his normal developmental stage if the entire family had not worked together.

Mending Family Systems

Not only are children engaged in processes of personality, emotional and social development, but their development is also significantly dependent upon the functioning and adaptive abilities of their family systems. The family system is ideally one of stability, love and protec-tion, where each child instinctively recognizes that ensuring his or her welfare is one of the primary tasks of the family. In responding to trauma, children and adolescents often take cues from their primary environment—their homes. When impacted by traumatic events, the family unit, in turn, needs to balance roles and responsibilities in a dynamic interplay between, among other areas, personality and gen-erational and cultural factors.

This is why it is so important to address traumatic repercus-sions in children from a family dynamic perspective. Such a perspec-tive becomes even more complex when a caretaker has also been directly involved in the traumatic event. The impact of a trauma may render the caretaker, and as a consequence, the family system, over-whelmed. If a parent, for instance, is experiencing acute anxiety and severe depression following the loss of a spouse, he or she may not have the emotional and coping resources necessary to help the family gain a new equilibrium.

Traumatic reactions in families generally undergo a metamor-phosis uniquely different than that of individuals. Working therapeu-tically with families and children often requires approaches notably different from working with one person. This is because each member of a family unit feels the impact of trauma differently and with varying degrees of intensity. One member's response to trauma may, in turn, change interactions between and among other family members. As adults of families often assume numerous roles such as parent, professional, student, daughter, son and spouse, traumatic events may affect one or more of these roles. I have seen children who attempted to take on caretaker roles for their parents who had suddenly lost spouses. Inappropriate roles like this inevitably stunt the growth of children and limit their ability to reach developmental milestones. Such shifts in role definition can lead to unbalanced and ultimately unhealthy family dynamics. Family systems can enter cycles of learned helplessness; consequently, subsequent challenges facing these families are met with more feelings of helplessness.

Post-traumatic phenomena in the family can lead to the loss of equilibrium within the family system. A traumatized family needs help on several levels. On one level, I try to help family members deal with their individual responses to the event. I also try to determine if one or more persons within the family are being blamed for the traumatic event and work to reduce scapegoating. In addition, I assist the family in working with any changes in roles, tasks and responsibilities that have come about as direct or indirect results of the event. On still another level, enhancing already present mechanisms of coping or developing new coping strategies may be necessary.

In my work with families who have experienced life-altering events, I have found that many families have strong rebound mechanisms and more often than not can successfully pull together to deal with traumatic events. One family used the anniversary date of their trauma to give thanks to each other and thus introduced a new family tradition that will likely be passed down to future generations. Another family spent the anniversary date of their trauma helping those who were less fortunate by volunteering at soup kitchens and children's hospitals. Yet, it is also not unusual for families to seek help in recovering from anniversary depressions. By their nature, the anniversary of traumatic events provokes families to emotionally distressing levels with which they need help coping.

My work with families in the aftermath of numerous traumatic events, including car accidents, sexual abuse, natural disasters affecting communities, incidents of general abuse and neglect as well as those recovering from 9/11, has shown me that each family must seek its own way of recovering. Additionally, in working with families who had to provide court testimony on multiple occasions or had to face the perpetrators of their traumas in open court, I have frequently seen post-traumatic stress reactions. When dealing with families, one must take into effect the duration of trauma, behavior during the event, grief and loss, senses of helplessness, exposure to death and the scope of the traumas. Each family comes to the event with its own unique set of traditions, family beliefs and roles. Therefore, each family must find its own unique way to a path of recovery.

Restoration of Family Unity

After a trauma, restoring family unity is vital. In many instances my role as a therapist has been to help alleviate any ongoing potential danger and then to engage all family members in initiating healthy responses to the trauma. The alleviation of potential danger may be to simply help the family seek shelter if the trauma is one of a natural disaster such as an earthquake or hurricane. Personal safety should always take precedence over any other intervention. Counseling can begin only after safety is secured.

Like individuals, families as units will experience and must cope with the shock, fear and anxiety that typically accompany tragedy. Assessing the losses suffered by the family as a result of the event is also crucial. For example, if an older sister died suddenly, the loss for the sibling might be the loss of a lifelong confidant. However, for a young child, the loss might be for a sister who can no longer take her on outings. For the parents, the death might mean the loss of aspirations they once had for their daughter. In this sense, losses may ultimately mean that certain characteristics of the deceased or roles once performed by the deceased may be eliminated or assumed by another family member. In the above example, another sibling or cousin or aunt may begin to take the young child on outings.

Families may also engage in reactive behavior that can send each individual into a tailspin. In family dynamics, how each member behaves invariably influences the behavior of every other family member. For instance, if there are two children in a family and one dies, and the parents behave as if the deceased child never existed, the surviving child has very limited outlets through which he or she can express loss or other feelings about the deceased sibling.

During the immediate crisis period after a trauma within a family, it is important to attempt to derail destructive patterns of handling the event while also working to capitalize on the positive coping mechanisms already in place within the family. In addition, in order to obtain crisis stabilization, each member of the family must be involved. Each must communicate to the others how the tragedy has impacted his or her life. Rather than denying loss, frustration, anger and other emotions experienced following tragedy, these feelings should be acknowledged as real. In this way, the family can work to regain hope and resilience. Early on in the process, it is important to remember how the family functioned prior to its trauma. In this way, the family's best strategies for coping can be identified and brought into the open so they can be used in the aftermath of trauma.

When a member of the family talks about his or her individual response to the traumatic event in the presence of the other family members, it also reframes the event so that the family can work through the issues together and help each other cope and problem-solve.

I have found that in the midst of a crisis, some families "forget" past crisis-management skills. Recalling these strengths also allows the family to externalize the event in a way that does not cripple the family's ability to use its combined resources. This stage ultimately allows the family to gather up and mobilize all its resources, both within the home and through such networks as support groups.

When the crisis period ends, the family is faced with the task of reorganization. In this stage, the family may need to reassign tasks that were derailed as a result of the trauma. For instance, the father may need to change his work schedule in order to take his children to their new school after the death of a mother. The family may also need to establish new goals. It is in this stage that family members need to regain a sense of order in their lives and develop skills that may be utilized in the event of any future crises.

When the family begins to actively engage in proactive behavior, I find it best to shift from being a therapist to being a coach. As a coach, I acknowledge the behaviors and contributions of each member of the family that resulted in positive solutions. Highlighting the family as the source of these helpful changes encourages families who have been through trauma to continue to forge ahead as a cohesive unit. Hopefully, if your family has been through a traumatic event, you too will reach this positive stage of recovery and healing, as have many families with whom I've worked.

The Miller Family

One family which attained this healing was the Millers. The family unit was comprised of two parents and two children, Darren, age seven, and Nathaniel, age fourteen. They had all been asleep on the second floor of their home when the smoke detectors went off. Since they had practiced what they would do in case of fire, all made it out of the house physically unharmed.

However, the fire spread quickly and required the combined efforts of three firehouses to extinguish the flames. As the family watched their house burn, both boys appeared to be in shock, while their parents appeared anxious and agitated. Mr. Miller kept pacing in front of the house while Mrs. Miller alternated between crying and making attempts to call other members of her extended family on her cell phone. After some time, a community resource agency worker arrived and offered the Millers food, clothing and shelter. At this point Mr. Miller's parents arrived. They politely declined other offers of shelter, but accepted a list of other community resources in the area.

According to the Millers, the initial two weeks following the fire seemed almost surreal. Mrs. Miller noted that she found herself, "stopping in my tracks and seriously wondering why I was not in my own home." Mr. Miller reported, going through the motions of getting the family resituated. "I remember contacting the bank, requesting new credit cards and other things of that type. Yet, I often felt like I was play-acting in a bad movie," he said. Both parents also noted when they called me that the children were more withdrawn and, like their parents, were complaining of poor sleep and nightmares.

When I met with the children, they spoke about the impact of the trauma from their perspectives. Both children talked of being scared that it would happen again and said, like their parents, that they missed cherished objects lost and their home itself. They also voiced their concern that, "things will never be the same again," and they were very worried about their parents' safety and well-being. They also feared that their grandparents would eventually, "get tired of us and then we will be homeless."

In addition to reassuring the children regarding their fears, I commended the entire family on their foresight in preparing for such an event. They all seemed to have forgotten the skills they used to survive and the calm in which they carried out their plan to exit their house during the fire. As we worked together I tried to instill hope for the future by initiating discussion about what had already been done to rebalance the family unit and what obstacles they had successfully overcome in the past. We also worked together to determine what resources would be helpful in this particular situation and whether there were new tools that might help them in regaining family equilibrium.

The parents agreed to reestablish chores, homework time, bedtimes and other formally established house rules. Following several more sessions along these lines, the family was able to consider how it would function in the light of past trauma. They established new goals that included taking fire prevention classes. The parents also decided that the children would be an integral part of their house-hunting experience, which would offer the children a greater sense of control. This family, I am happy to report, put their goals into action, eventually found a new home and went forward with renewed hope.

Life-altering events challenge us all to rise above our ordeals and to find opportunities for life-affirming confirmation within our struggles. When children and families are involved, these challenges are multifold. Yet, by the same token, the support of family and other social networks may allow the burden to be shared and more easily managed by a cohesive group. Families can be a source of hope and strength. Often I have seen and counseled them as they struggle valiantly against the destructive tide of trauma, emerging from its depths closer and stronger as a family.

Chapter 9 Resilience Tips

- Set up a family meeting to talk about the impact of the event from each family member's perspective and ways to heal.
- Reach out to family members who seem withdrawn or extremely distraught.
- Maintain or recreate appropriate family roles (i.e., parent, child, spouse, etc.).
- Allow extended family and friends to support the family.
- Recognize when professional help or support groups may be needed and actively seek such help.
- Reinstitute family chores, rituals and rules.
- Establish new family goals.
- Plan how the family will put goals into action.
- Meet to commend each other on successes and discuss ways to handle failure and crises.

Exercise for Parents and Other Caretakers

Being alert to any changes in a child's behavior or mood in the days to weeks following a traumatic event can be instrumental in helping that child cope with the event. Below is a list of some of the more common reactions of children and adolescents. Note which ones your child or children display.

1. Regressive behaviors (e.g., bed-wetting, clinging, whimpering, thumb-sucking)
2. Reenactments of aspects of the event
3. Sad, withdrawn, and/or depressed moods
4. Irritability or angry outbursts
5. Restless or agitated behavior
6. Seeming easily startled and hyper-alert
7. Expression of irrational fears
8. Avoidance of reminders or cues related to the event
9. Experiencing nightmares or frequent memories of the event
10. Avoidance of school or peers
11. Physical complaints (e.g., stomach aches, headaches, etc.)
12. Aggressive or defiant behavior
13. Changes in grooming or dressing habits
14. Truant and/or antisocial behaviors (stealing, damaging property, etc.)

ALSO:

- Talk about the event with children
- Provide ongoing reassurance
- Return to normal routine as soon as possible
- If behaviors persist for more than a few weeks, seek support from a mental health professional.

It is common for a family to feel overwhelmed by a crisis and may feel at a loss as to how to regain family stability. The following exercise is geared toward helping the family regain its balance.

1. Make a list of previous challenges that the family has faced:

    _____

    _____

    _____

    _____

2. Write down how each challenge was resolved:

    _____

    _____

    _____

    _____

3. Decide which solutions from the list above can be used in the current situation. The solution can be exactly the same or a modified version. List those solutions below:

    _____

    _____

    _____

    _____

4. Are there other alternatives that could work in the current situation? If so, list them below:

    _____

    _____

    _____

    _____

5. List all social supports available to the family (e.g. extended family members, friends and community resources):

    _____

    _____

    _____

    _____

List family goals in order of importance and decide which steps are needed to reach each goal.

Goal #1: _____

Steps to reach this goal:

_____

_____

_____

_____

Goal #2: _____

Steps to reach this goal:

_____

_____

_____

_____

Goal #3: _____

Steps to reach this goal:

_____

_____

_____

_____

Assign steps to appropriate family members.

Family member: _____

Task:_____

Family member: _____

Task:_____

Family member: _____

Task:_____

Family member: _____

Task:_____

Family member: _____

Task:_____

Continue down the list of goals, utilizing your response to items #3 and #4 above and your list of social supports.

Chapter 10

Transitions to Recovery:
Memorabilia, Anniversaries
and Other Reflective Remembrances

Over time as I have worked with survivors, I saw that memorabilia seemed to serve as a therapeutic anchor for emotions, allowing some survivors the opportunity to moor themselves nostalgically between regret and happy remembrance. The act of attachment to a particular object appears to counter the natural tendency to deny trauma, making room for and allowing affirmation of both positive and more troublesome emotions. When they are ready, survivors are able to "remember" by looking at mementos of the past including old letters, newspaper clippings, a photo album, a trunk in the attic and other keepsakes. As I attended more closely to this phenomenon, I started to ponder: What does memorabilia symbolize for individual survivors? What do particular objects reveal or signify to a person?

In my talks with survivors they revealed to me that memorabilia has been emotionally very evocative for them. Corki confided, "I have a statue, pictures, books and pins. These things show me what's in my heart. They are my remembrances, part of my history. These tokens help me remember the good times and make me feel better." Liz shared with me, "I have a tee shirt. The tee shirt came from one of the women I met in the battered woman's shelter the day I arrived. I think this tee shirt means the most to me, because it came from the heart." Mara related, "I have at least three pins, a key ring, and a poster. The pins mean the most to me, because every time I look at a pin I flash back to the positive times." Gale told me she keeps her dead child's stuffed teddy bear under the blanket on her bed. As revealed by these survivors, memorabilia appears to act as a personal touchstone, helping to remind and retain the positive memories of the person or life lost.

Sometimes the survivors who began to collect memorabilia viewed their collection as concrete remembrances of personal and family histories to be passed down to their children and their children's children; others have been able to tap into feelings of humility and honor as they began to see that their lives before their traumas had richness that had been overlooked in their suffering. It is as if the act of remembering allows individuals to experience their memories in varied textures. Symbolically, memorabilia seems very meaningful to survivors as it allows such open recollection to become part of their worldview. It helps them connect to life's brilliance and vitality and allows them the opportunity to give attention and articulation to the subjective emotional self rather than only to the reasoning self. These objects are therefore powerful reminders of humanity and the happiness and sorrow in their past lives, because they have the ability to stir the soul. They place the survivor into a new relationship with the world that is no longer detached from the heart.

Waking Dreams

In many ways, memorabilia seems like a tangible dream upon which to gaze during waking hours, allowing the dreamer to feel closer to the people, places and things that give sustenance to that which had been deemed lost and now was rediscovered on a level beyond normal perception. The dreams evoked by memorabilia allow the dreamer the opportunity to imagine and relive other states of being. Survivors have spoken to me about memorabilia symbolizing the intangibles of life, like interconnectivity and intimacy. As they involved themselves emotionally with these connections to the "other," it was as if they became more expansive and more personally expressive. This attention to something outside themselves was allowing them, paradoxically, to gain a greater depth of character.

All survivors seem to feel this acutely. Therese related, "I always wear at least one pin every day. I think wearing a pin is the least I can do to show support for families of the fallen and I also want people never to forget."

Robert says, "I have a piece of wall tile from the site which reminds me of the destruction of the building, loss of life and those who paid the ultimate price. This wall tile has symbolic meaning for me. It has helped with the healing process, because I knew I would never go to the site, but at least I have a piece of it with me."

Alyce noted, "I have old photos, pins and tee shirts that I got from the job. They mean a lot to me because they represent the sense of "family" at work and strengthened my connection to my fellow employees."

Janet recalled, "I have a homemade birthday card that my murdered father made for me. I treasure the card, because it is both funny and loving and symbolizes those traits I most admired in him."

As for me, I asked my mother to buy me a series of photo essay books about the tragedy of 9/11. I am a person who usually brings a camera on vacation and forgets to take pictures. Nevertheless, memorabilia related to my own trauma has become a snapshot of a memorialized time in my life, an extension of who I am today. My collection somehow conveys for me what language cannot articulate. Other survivors of different traumas have told me that by simply gazing upon their remembrances, their presence was powerful enough to convey their significance. In pursuit of a deeper integration of my own trauma, I have accumulated dozens of pins, photographs and posters.

Two pictures of the physical site, taken by a colleague several days before the event have become treasures. One of the two photographs was taken from an office window and was focused on the Empire State Building. In this photograph, the sky is a pale blue with billowy white clouds. The image spans clear across to the East River. The second photograph was taken from street level. The picture was taken with the camera angled upward; trees shade the lower portion of the building. I feel comforted when I see the buildings stand majestically, exuding a soulful quality that is colored by my own experience that tragic day.

Trauma Settings

Along with memorabilia, sites of trauma, crime scenes, cemeteries and other settings associated with the ordeals often evoke strong feelings and memories. For those who are going through a period of denial, these settings may bring them face to face with acknowledgment that the event really happened. For others, such sights are emotional triggers and may set off a spasm of grief. For still others, it is a rite of passage and some gain comfort from the visit. Remember, go when you are ready. Bring someone empathetic if you feel the need for support. Don't feel you must go, for instance, to the cemetery frequently if you don't want to, but visit when and if it consoles you. If you have been a victim of sudden trauma and feel that returning to the scene will aid in your recovery, determine how this will best be done.

As the months passed after 9/11, some of the World Trade Center survivors I had been guiding and monitoring felt that it was emotionally unbearable to even think of visiting the place of their trauma. Others, however, reported a sense of readiness to visit Ground Zero. Some of these latter survivors requested that I accompany them on their first trips back to the site. As more and more requests of this nature were voiced, I was forced to face the fact that I too had not been near the site since I the day I lived through its unimaginable death and devastation. Was I ready to go back there? I mulled over this question for a while until I finally decided that I would visit the site with the person closest to me. I would go as if I were a person revisiting an old home.

My closest friend and I first viewed the area from the twentieth floor of a building overlooking the site. From this vantage point it was easier to see where buildings, stores and other landmarks used to be. As I gazed down, the enormity of the catastrophe could not be denied. The sheer size of the footprint, the number of people busily working in its pit and the constant bustle within the general environment of the site spoke volumes.

As we made our way down the makeshift ramp that led directly onto the site, I recalled spending summer lunch hours outdoors in the plaza, listening to afternoon music performances. I remembered being there before the tragedy with my friend beside me and at other times with my younger sister who had visited with me during her summer breaks from college. I glanced to my right and in a flash, I remembered a lunch date with a friend who still worked several blocks away. I looked back to the two of us sitting in a small park nearby, eating lunch together. I smiled as I recalled her putting down her sandwich as she reached for her soft drink only to have a seeing-eye dog suddenly gulp down her entire sandwich in one bite. I remembered laughing at the comically stunned expression she wore at that moment.

Returning to the present, I surveyed the site. It was mind-boggling to see that only very small piles of the destroyed buildings remained. As we stood there, awe and sadness coalesced as I reflected on that day. What lay before me were the tangible remains of a catastrophe I had personally suffered, attesting to its appalling reality. Yet with all that, reality gained its proper perspective. Yes, tragedy occurred, but positive things took place here as well.

Therese shared the story of her visit to the site with me, saying, "I went to the site with people I felt comfortable with. Even though it was extremely upsetting and the devastation was overwhelming, I was glad I went. I think memorials and other events of remembrance help me mourn, because it shows me that I'm not the only one feeling distraught. It lets me see that grief is affecting other people as well. I think both private and public mourning helps me work through my grief in a healthy way. Now when I reflect on the site, it brings back another set of memories and that is of the buildings during their construction."

Joyce confided in me, saying, "I first went to the site about three weeks after the tragedy. I don't think it hit me yet back then. I went again about six months later and it helped me accept what happened."

Many survivors have spoken of how visiting a site physically was yet another transition point on the road to their recovery. Merely being at the site was an undeniable confirmation of the reality of their adversity and an event that therefore had to be accepted for what it was.

Anniversaries, Memorial Services and Other Time-Markers

Funerals, anniversaries, memorials and other time-marked remembrances are other events that stir the cauldron of memories and emotions for people who have suffered sudden tragedy. Although for some, going to these time-markers is a rite of passage, for others, attendance at these events results in emotional overload and searing grief. During the weeks leading up to the anniversary of a traumatic event, survivors typically report increases in distressing behavioral and emotional symptoms. Along with these increased symptoms may come feelings of reliving the trauma. Some survivors suffer sleep disturbances, fatigue, generalized anxiety, distractibility, irritability and changes in mood. Some become more tearful and melancholy, while others feel agitated or restless. Although commonalities exist, each individual invariably feels these reactions in his or her own distinctive way.

If you are faced with such potent milestones, consider it to be normal if you experience grief reactions. Time markers should be seen as partly healing and partly grieving occasions. Mourning through various rituals, whether church services, memorial services or family remembrances, may be helpful in focusing your grief reactions, therefore allowing you to find greater control of the aftereffects of trauma. This view lets you grieve freely while allowing you to rejoice in related positive memories. This perspective also gives permission to formally acknowledge pain without feeling guilt that you continue to grieve.

It is also helpful to think about what steps can be taken to better cope with specific time markers. Unlike the day of the traumatic event, you as a survivor can exert some control by preparing for the anniversary day. In the end, engaging in those activities that are emotionally tolerable and comforting while at the same time determining the best way to honor the person who was lost or your own experience, will be most effective. It is also important to remind oneself that the process of mourning is ongoing and requires active engagement and acceptance of all emotional states.

I have found that social support aids many survivors. In essence, being with others feeling similarly may allow expressions of one's grief process. Before such a time marker comes up, think about what you will do on that date so that it does not creep up on you. But also be aware that you cannot plan for all the feelings that may occur. Be gentle with yourself.

When I underscored these insights to the survivors with whom I have worked over the years, many talked freely about the processes they were undergoing. For Mary, the one-year anniversary of her child's murder was a day filled with tears. "It was as if I was experiencing the frightening, painful news again," she said. "I had decided I wanted to go to Mass early that morning. I did, came home and cooked for the rest of my family. But I also cried all day."

Mary's anxiety, tearfulness and grief reactions had returned.

For her, as well as other trauma sufferers I have counseled, including families and survivors of September 11th, not only was the date difficult but the day laden with emotion. As Mary expressed to me, "It was a very sad day."

As we revisited Mary's grief, we carefully walked through the anniversary day as she had experienced it. I wanted Mary to express her feelings in order to short-circuit her attempts at avoidance, a defense mechanism in which Mary had previously been stuck. We talked about grief stages and how each stage exhibited an intertwined relationship with the traumatic experience. I told Mary that it was all right to feel her loss so acutely. We talked about her child and the dreams lost the day he died and said a prayer in remembrance of him.

A week before the anniversary of September 11th, Alyce reported impaired sleep. She was emotionally upset by a chance meeting with someone who had been strongly connected to her during the event but whom she had not seen since that day. She noted how other things had suddenly become more potent triggers for her. She was now afraid to acknowledge anything good about where she lived, fearing that it would bring misfortune to that place. As Alyce now acknowledged, a sunny day, as September 11th was, had also acted as a major trigger. *Was that why she sat home in the dark for several months?* I wondered.

I told Alyce that although there might have been an increase in her symptoms, it did not mean that she was faltering on the path to healing, but merely that strong triggers could engender equally strong reactions. We carefully reviewed her plans for the day and the positive aspects inherent in planning for reflection or activity or both. Upon review, Alyce decided that on the one-year anniversary she would go out of town and visit with her daughter.

For Carlos, extended periods of sadness and anxiety returned as the one-year mark of his wife's death in a car crash approached. We discussed what he had learned thus far in coping with and managing such symptoms and how he was much more prepared to deal with anxiety, tension and sadness than he was immediately following the event. We talked about the support system that remained available to him. I reinforced to him the concept of "one step at a time" and the benefits of being gentle with himself. "It will be helpful," I said, "if you acknowledge your sadness and anxiety as real but not as insurmountable." We then moved on to the issue of emotional control.

"What is controllable on the one-year anniversary?" I queried.
He paused and then said, "I can control what I do that day." We talked about the ways in which he could acknowledge the loss, cope with the emotions attached to his trauma and then do what felt good to do in the moment. In the end, Carlos decided that going to church with his ten-year-old daughter to reflect upon, remember and honor his wife, and then spend the afternoon with his daughter at a park the family had enjoyed was what he wanted and needed to do.

For Brandon, a 9/11 survivor, as the second anniversary of September 11th approached, his fear of going to his job on that day returned. Was the anxiety related to his job the sum projection of his fear, grief, loss and feeling of helplessness? We examined these themes from every angle, direction and dimension. Brandon also talked with his wife, friends and extended family members about his lack of a work identity since the trauma. He wrote a list of pros and cons related to his job. He looked deep inside himself for the right answer and then probed deeper still. Eventually, he agreed to suspend reflection on his work identity until the anniversary passed. We then focused on what would be best for him to do that day. Together, we decided that Brandon would visit the cemetery where some of those lost now rested and then spend the rest of the day with his wife and children eating lunch out and engaging in a leisure activity.

For Sara, the upcoming anniversary of her husband's murder three years earlier encroached upon her and she experienced heart palpitations, greater generalized anxiety and acute insomnia. Yet Sara continued to reach out for help; practiced anxiety management techniques; spent time with her prayer group; and confided her feelings to her sister. While meeting with Sara, I demonstrated other deep breathing exercises she could practice. Sara also attended EMDR (Eye Movement Desensitization and Reprocessing) sessions and reported that the evening following her initial EMDR appointment she slept soundly through the night prior to the anniversary for the first time since the trauma.

Nevertheless, the day of the anniversary was very emotional for Sara. But instead of withdrawing from others, she talked about her feelings with those close to her. As we had discussed, Sara spent the anniversary morning in church and the remainder of the day with her sister, children and grandchildren. "We had a little party," she said with tenderness in her eyes. She told me that, overall, she was feeling more in control and felt fortified with strategies to manage her anxiety. She appeared to have a stronger sense of self. Sara was learning ways to be vulnerable and in that vulnerability, ironically, was stronger for it. She was becoming more comfortable seeking help and had learned that seeking help was not a sign of weakness but rather a sign of courage. The process of seeking help itself offered an opportunity to experience loving support.

Steff, another 9/11 survivor, and I talked about his feelings and thoughts surrounding the one-year anniversary. He articulated a sense of confidence and ease. As we talked, I realized that Steff had returned to the emotional space he occupied during and in the immediate aftermath of his trauma—his strong desire to be there for others if needed. In the end, he decided to go to work on the anniversary and spend the day in the company of those who also survived that day.

Having additionally suffered the death of her father-in-law and a car accident in which she sustained neck injuries, for Mara, the approaching anniversary of the terrorist attack on the World Trade Center was exceedingly difficult. The approaching milestone was again pushing her down into another depressive episode. Mara reported that she made a visit to the site of the trauma. She told me that afterwards she "began to cry nonstop again," and to "not care about anything." Again, she no longer wanted to be responsible for anything, including her daughter and significant other. She spoke of being plagued by guilt, grief and loss. "I'm angry at the world. I also feel guilty and ask myself, 'Why not me?' I feel like I can't be happy, like it would be dishonoring the memories of those who died," she said. Mara also believed that she should not make any plans for the future. "I don't care—live or not live." In the end, Mara decided to seek a psychiatric consultation and her medication was subsequently increased.

We then began meeting frequently to further process her trauma. We talked of the trauma in the context of her guilt and feelings of inadequacy. We reviewed how trauma, by its nature, leaves one with feelings of helplessness and powerlessness. In spite of such normal feelings, I insisted that she attempt to accomplish at least one task a day. I empathized, encouraged and reinforced every single small step she made toward recovery. I asked that she follow through on each and every resource and support available to her. Luckily, she did and firmly stepped forward on the path of healing.

Re-establishing Balance

Each survivor I have known takes a different path in getting through such milestones. Some feel that going to work will be too painful, while others look forward to the support of their coworkers. Some do not want to participate in memorials, others find them comforting and necessary for their own healing process. Some survivors feel that attending religious services to remember loved ones lost will be helpful while many others wish to spend the day with family members or friends. Still others want to spend the anniversary date walking on a beach or in a quiet, secluded area. Some use the day to remember their own friends and family members, social supports and the personal resilience that have helped in the past. Many survivors engage in quiet reflection—the pain of personal loss, what happened, where they were emotionally and where they are now.

In essence, anniversaries and other remembrances bring us face to face with issues of attachment that may be centered on a person, our future, our beliefs or our ideals. Anniversaries are poignant occasions to reflect on these attachments, particularly if those anniversaries commemorate events involving the loss of life. They can compel us to contemplate the complexities of our attachments to the person or people lost. These reflections can be confusing during periods so laden with emotion. This is especially true if we are striving to move beyond a specific stage of grief at that time. Then our reflections may center on a particular stage, such as anger, which may be driven by thoughts for a lost loved one."Why didn't he take better physical care of himself?" "If she only had been somewhere else, I wouldn't be in such turmoil."

Thoughts of personal failure may also exist. In a similar fashion, for those who feel they have lost an ideal such as trust and innocence, anniversaries may fuel emotions that are the antithesis of such ideals. It is important for you if you are a survivor to accept all the complexities of attachment without judgment. Keep in mind that it is better to feel the complexity of life than to live in an internal world without affect. It is important to note that all emotions "just are." There is no need to feel guilty, selfish or miserable about what you feel, but try not to hold on to one particular emotion, set each emotion free as the next one is felt. On the other hand, remember that just as one is capable of feeling anxiety or anger, one is just as capable of feeling peace and happiness.

On the first anniversary of September 11th, I made plans to maintain telephone contact with my own family members and close friends. I also decided to spend the early part of the day in my office in order to be available to any survivors who became overwhelmed. My afternoon, however, was spent in quiet remembrance of those I knew who had perished. In the evening, I attended a memorial service at a local park with my neighbors. I also reflected privately over the events of the past year. I chose to spend the second anniversary in a similar way.

Through the years I've counseled survivors of life's tragedies. I am humbled by our minds' ability to withstand the onslaught of images of pain, destruction and death. As I step back and view those I've counseled, I notice the ways in which the mind passively takes in the particulars of a traumatic event and how it struggles in the aftermath to understand what occurred. I accept that the mind dips in and out of shock, uncertainty and grief, allowing itself, when needed, respites from self-analysis through distraction and, yes, denial—all in the service of self-preservation and regeneration. I have found that at times, the mind can surprise you with its ability to connect the minutest of images, sounds, and smells to past traumas which then ignites other images, rendering you a little nervous, and perhaps in awe about its abilities and powers. At the same time, I have realized in reflecting on my own trauma that the mind soothes as it offers healing connections. Over time and with the insight and counsel I have had, and which I wish for you, the opportunity to integrate the experience in both a neutral and emotional way and to discover within yourself an intrinsic hardiness and resilience will come to you as it has to me.

Chapter 10 Resilience Tips

- Assess whether mood, thought, behavior and physical health change on the same date, month, year, birthday, wedding anniversary or other time-marker related to your trauma. This reexperiencing or reliving of the event is known as an "anniversary reaction" and can span the complete spectrum of emotions, behaviors, thoughts and physical reactions. Be aware that all of your reactions are NORMAL and are to be expected.
- Be aware: anniversaries and other time markers can cause flashback emotions for trauma sufferers and other survivors.
- On anniversaries of trauma it may help you to find a quiet, private space and hold or touch pictures, letters, newspaper clippings, keepsake or other such memorabilia that reflects your loss.
- Picture the person lost or yourself if you have suffered trauma during a happy occasion. What was the occasion? Where did it occur? What were you wearing? What caused the feeling of happiness?
- Recall another enjoyable experience that invoked similar feelings of happiness or joy.
- If you have lost a loved one, ask yourself what were the personality traits that you really connected with in this person. What parts of this person do you miss? Try to emulate those traits.
- Recognize that your anguished reactions are temporary and typically fade following the time-marker.
- View anniversary reactions as part mourning and part healing.
- Engage in both remembrance and life-affirming activities.
- Remember that on your healing journey you have gained knowledge about how you experience trauma and this knowledge can be used to help you cope with anniversary reactions.
- Allow yourself to be with others or to be alone. Do whatever comforts you.
- Decide how you will spend the anniversary before the date arrives.
- If you are having suicidal thoughts, it is imperative that you seek professional assistance immediately.

EXERCISE

TIME-MARKER PLANNER

Anniversaries and other time-markers related to a trauma are often difficult periods for survivors. While strong emotions are to be expected, planning for the day may help alleviate excessive suffering. Complete the exercise below.

Who Would I Like to Be with on That Day?

Think about a person or people you feel would make the day more tolerable for you. Choose a friend, family member or a member of your support group if you belong to one. Ask that person to set aside time for you on that day and decide when and where to meet.

Name(s): _____   _____

Meeting time: _____

Meeting place: _____

What Do I Want to Do That Day
to Honor Those Lost but Affirm Life?

For example, lighting a candle in remembrance of a lost loved one can be an "honor" event and spending the afternoon playing with a child or grandchild can be a "life-affirming event."

	Honor Event	Life-affirming Event
MORNING:		
AFTERNOON:		
EVENING:		

Chapter 11

Crisis May
Unmask Opportunity

Whenever I see a new trauma patient in my private practice, I end our first session by giving the person a sheet of paper. On it are the Chinese symbols for crisis and opportunity. When the client invariably notices that the symbols are the same, I say, "Yes. That is because out of crisis opportunity may come." I tell the survivor, who is usually surprised, that though in the aftermath of trauma it seems only shock and grief are possible, as their healing journey continues, self-awareness, resilience and self-growth rise. I cannot recall even one person who looked even partially convinced by my words in those first sessions. I also cannot recall one patient who looked unconvinced at the end of our work together. It may also reassure you to be aware that over time hundreds of thousands of survivors do go on with their lives and do learn to successfully cope with the traumas they have suffered. In the past I have seen that such a realization has led many survivors to find their own paths of healing.

Trauma's Hidden Opportunities

Time and time again I have coached survivors as they seek out and then nurture the life-enhancing tools that trauma can deceitfully hide from them. This is not to suggest that after an individual has coped successfully with a tragic event and the feelings of grief, sorrow, intense anger and injustice which may come afterward, his or her life is guaranteed to feel totally complete. Rather, the message here is that although in the beginning one may feel overcome by shock and grief, as one copes more and more successfully, opportunities for self renewal appear. In this revitalization period, many survivors are able to reincorporate some of the positive aspect of their lives before trauma and reach a new level of self-empowerment.

Surviving, Striving and Succeeding

Two years after her trauma, one survivor I counseled, Alyce, had reached the point where she could see these opportunities in her own life. Her mood had changed from despairing to hopeful. She noted that her life was "going very well" and every day she strove to get stronger. Alyce no longer sat in the dark, slept eighteen hours a day or isolated herself from friends and family. She is now working full time again, maintaining her social support network and has solid plans for the future. Alyce is facing her feelings of anxiety about the outside world and has decided that she will no longer be paralyzed by fear.

As the psychological triggers which repeatedly plunged Alyce back into the past lost their potency through her hard work and motivation to live a quality life, another potentially distressing trigger arose for Alyce. Unexpectedly, and for the first time since her tragedy, Alyce saw another person who had been there. Upon seeing him, she became ecstatic and she hugged him for a long time, remembering the experiences they shared. Months earlier, a similar occasion had sent Alyce reeling back into despondency. The outcome of this chance meeting was one illustration that she had successfully integrated two opposing sets of emotions. She could feel both sadness for her loss and joy for what remained.

As Alyce said to me, "Seeking help was a very important step for me. Even though I initially resisted treatment, I found that once I committed to it, therapy has been indispensable. Also, coming back to work full-time confirmed that I could get back to somewhat of a regular existence and it made me feel more normal. Revisiting my spirituality also helped me better cope.

"I feel more able to tackle things head-on. I have a stronger sense of self-worth and have become more assertive as a result. It was a very difficult time for me, but it could have been worse and I am thankful to be given another day."

Alyce told me that helping her to become introspective was the contribution I made to her recovery. "You made me look at me, the person," she said. "I had stopped being me. I had stopped living and was masking my actions. You helped redefine who I am in a positive way. I'm making more down time to relax and define who I am. It's a work in progress, this getting in touch with myself and I'm still creating it."

Morgan, another survivor, has told me, "Psychotherapy, medication and the EMDR sessions have been very helpful in helping me onto a path to recovery. Reading has been extremely calming and listening to music has helped me, too. The aftermath and my struggle to cope was a very trying time, a frightening period, yet I continue to hope and strive for peace, control and safety."

Today Corki's face is less strained and she can now talk about the event without feeling hysterical. Although she sometimes still cries when emotionally triggered and experiences sporadic anxiety, Corki no longer denies or avoids these emotional states as she did for many months. Overall, she feels stronger, with a strong support system in place and is no longer consumed by fear and anxiety.

Bob speaks often of the higher level of self-awareness he now enjoys, noting that he has not felt so much like himself in years! He said, "Finding my way out of the denial of my trauma was a major, major step forward. Talking about and working through my injuries actually helped me find something even better—self-confidence. I didn't realize that I had lost my self-confidence until I looked at who I had become over the years. I was merely some guy who worked and supported his family. I was terrified when the injury forced me off this comfortable but unfulfilling path. Now I feel much closer to my wife and son. I think this is so because I sought and acted on parts of me that I had buried since they were no longer part of this rigid road I had taken."

Bob told me I played an important role in his recovery by my insistence that he not only address his trauma but also look beyond it. If I could speak to you personally I would ask you to do this, too.

If, like Joyce, you continue to mourn due to suffering from multiple traumas, I hope it is comforting to know that like her, you can move through the process of recovery. Feeling more accepting of their loss and grateful for their lives, Joyce now visits her sons graves regularly to place flowers upon them. While Joyce continues to struggle to be assertive, I encourage every attempt that she makes. In fact, she now tells me when she needs to talk; by this behavior she asserts that what she has to say matters. As she puts it, "I'm telling it like it is now." Recently she said, "Surviving the event has made me feel special and blessed. It has also made me realize that I can handle a lot of adversity."

This pride in survival is a quality other survivors come to know and appreciate.

Similarly, Brandon said, "It was an extremely hard time. The search for myself—who I really am, and what I want to do with my life—was a very uncomfortable feeling. Keeping busy and journaling was very helpful to me during this process. Through these things and meeting with my psychologist, I have learned a lot about myself.

"In my heart, when all is said and done, I feel my life will be better. I'm more family-oriented and not as reckless as I was before. I believe in myself and trust my inner self. I have the faith in me that I never had before."

For Therese, "In the end, accepting that I could not rely on my old strategies for coping was an important lesson. The event made me feel stronger overall, because it made me realize that it takes a hell of a lot to bring me down. I feel defiant in the face of my trauma. As I reflect, I see both good and bad things coming out of the event. The good things were that it brought us together for a time and it prompted me to open my eyes, to be wiser and smarter forever."

How happy I was to see that Therese's face exuded calmness and newfound wisdom as she spoke. The juxtaposition of Therese's attitude in the immediate aftermath of her traumatic experience and now, nearly two years later, is astounding. When I'd first met her, Therese could see no future for herself and avoided life entirely. Now Therese looks forward and embraces life. On the last day we spoke, she filled my office with a sense of purpose and an inner strength that was infectious.

Carol, another survivor whom I counseled, said, "My eventual commitment to working with you to understand myself is the key to my growth. I call it growth, because I now believe that I stopped growing the first time I was abused. At that exact moment, I began to live in a stunted world where I treated everyone as if they were my mother or my abusers."

Today Carol has accepted the past and made the transition from child to adult. She has integrated her trauma and is now able to engage in adult relationships. She no longer vacillates between seeking interpersonal interactions and summarily dismissing those she engages in such encounters, lest they hurt her before she can reject them.

Antoinette, another survivor, has, as the year following her trauma proceeded on to the next, continued to heal. Most assuredly, bouts of anxiety and moments of depression still occur for her, but these periods are less intense and fewer in number.

Recently Antoinette talked with me about learning how to accept situations and people as they are while concentrating on how she can be a better person. She told me that she now is committed to seeking help if that is what she needs. She has also said me that she is learning to slow down, to listen and trust her inner voice and to no longer second-guess herself—a tendency that often left her unable to act. Antoinette has made positive changes and decisions and is proud of the fact that she now is doing well in school. She wakes up every morning determined to live her day to the fullest.

Reflecting on her journey along the healing path Antoinette says, "I chose individual psychotherapy and medication to help me through. Also getting full body massages, attending women's retreats, going to church, and being with my children made me feel better.

"I think another important thing that helped me cope was coming back to work. It helped me realize that I was capable of getting back to some version of normal. I see time now as an opportunity for renewal and growth. I learned a lot about myself. I learned that there was strength inside me because even though the event and its aftermath knocked me down, I didn't stay down. The event made me realize that I am resilient and have the strength to get back up.

For Mara, treatment was helpful because, as she said, "Individual psychotherapy and medication have been key in helping me feel better. Getting help has made me stronger, because I have learned how to grieve better. I have also learned that it is okay to grieve and to have emotions and not judge yourself harshly because you are grieving."

Today Mara is working, spending time with her family and friends and is committed to the task of normalizing her life. While on earlier occasions she struggled to leave her home even for an hour and was terrified of large crowds, Mara now attends plays and has even sung karaoke in front of a large audience.

Liz noted that her recovery has been aided by multiple supports, including therapy. "Support systems like my minister, husband, children, psychologists and prayer groups helped me to cope. Learning to manage my anxiety, using positive self-talk daily and going through EMDR was instrumental to my recovery process. Without this support it would have been unbearable for me. The way people came to my aid gave me the strength to help myself. It enabled me to take control of *me*. I am now better able to cope with everything in life.

"When I reflect on the experience, I think of how it was a very trying time. It was mentally challenging. There is no comparison to the amount of stress, grief, anger, anxiety and fear I experienced. And with all of this weighing on me, I had to maintain my sanity. It was all so profound. Yet I feel better about my future. I feel hopeful that I can make it through and cope if something else was to happen. I also found renewed faith in God. I had to stop focusing on those who were lost that day and rejoice for the many that were saved. I became comfortable in my belief in God's will and then became able to focus on getting better, for me."

Liz has continued to make progress and reads positive affirmations on a daily basis. She has learned to delay responding to requests that potentially could overburden her. While managing her symptoms is an ongoing process, Liz has redefined herself and her relationship to others. As Liz aptly said to me about her growing competence, "I feel more comfortable than ever before. My husband is so pleased about my progress. I'm also no longer scared or have sleeping problems." As she reflected further on our sessions together, she said, "From day one, you took control of me in a sense, because I was out of control. You helped me gain control of myself again. You were supportive and made me realize that my trauma was not something I brought on myself."

Janet feels therapy has also been very helpful. As her healing journey has progressed, I have seen Janet continue to grow as a person and her emotional ties to others have deepened. "I feel my dad's presence in everything that I do. I can't help but feel that as I am moving forward and becoming who I am today, he is looking down on me in approval," she articulated. She also says that now she feels closer to her mother. As she confided to me, "I didn't realize that my being so angry that my father was killed, prevented me from knowing my own mother better."

During this trying period in her life, Janet has also tapped into her spiritual side. She reported to me that she has begun to learn more about her religion and has joined church groups. She has shared with me her feeling of renewed connection to God and the comfort that brings.

Steff talks with pride about his newfound commitment to his music and the positive relationships he has cultivated through perseverance, assertiveness and love. Steff is now very much focused on quality-of-life issues and how he can best bring joy and love to his life and the lives of others.

Ultimately, Steff has come to believe emphatically that the trauma itself has not made him stronger. Rather, in his opinion, the fundamental aspects that have supported his recovery are seeking outside help, coping and reintegrating the trauma into his life in positive ways.

He said, "I did some serious self reflection and felt propelled to act positively in my life. The event made me a better person today. The crisis turned into an opportunity for growth. It made me stronger to know that God has a plan for me. It has heightened my faith that things will get better.

"I know that I'm not over the trauma I suffered. It's still a tough road. It has certainly changed my perspective. But one thing it has made me is more resolved to make better use of my time and to start to implement and work toward those dreams, visions and passions that I believe are gifts from God, things that He wants me to do."

Post-traumatic Growth

At first glance, destructive trauma and self-growth may seem contradictory. Yet many survivors who have learned to cope with their hardships, trauma, adversities and losses, feel that the maturation, self-development and growth they've achieved are natural byproducts of their journeys to recovery. I also have found that the distressing reality of loss teaches us much about ourselves. Such survivors, a group in which I include myself, feel that the stress of these losses forces us to delve deep inside ourselves to cope with our pain. Integrating these traumatic events demands that we look critically at ourselves. As we have traveled further along the healing path, our trauma has revealed other dimensions that we would like to change—those things that may have impeded our recovery and self-improvement and which we may want to transform into something positive.

Of course, all survivors wish their traumas could have been avoided. Nonetheless, once sustained, survivors must, on their journeys to recovery, pursue growth if they are to heal. In this way, the meaning of "survivor" can encompass not only the coping aspects inherent in the term, but also the use of the challenge for self-realization.

One survivor who learned this lesson well was Joyce, whose seemingly innate ability to soothe and nurture others often led to an absence of such care for herself, culminating in a lack of self-confidence, a struggle to trust her instincts and a difficulty in asserting her own desires. Coping with the aftermath of her ordeal, Joyce began to seriously address these areas of conflict in her life.

Looking inward with intense scrutiny, she came to the conclusion that in the pursuit of self-actualization she needed to learn assertiveness. She determined that her instincts were generally good, but she realized that she needed to trust in herself more readily. She then acted on her desires, wishes and needs, which allowed the peace and calm that she desired to grow in her life. Joyce also made her wishes known to those around her and began to tell others what she needed—respect, consideration and kindness.

Please be reassured that many survivors with whom I have worked have reached a nexus of self-actualization as they healed in varying ways. As I've said before, just as each individual is unique, so too have been the paths they travel and the time they take to arrive at this revitalizing period of post-traumatic growth. I have observed that no matter when and how such growth occurs, each survivor has had to withstand barriers of pain and grief. The many who walk their unique paths to healing and recovery discover something larger than themselves, yet intrinsic to development of more introspective and compassionate selves.

Chapter 11 Resilience Tips

- Can you think of others who have survived trauma? Make a list of these heroes and the traumas they've lived through.
- Make a list of the impediments and difficulties they encountered along the way.
- Are there any clues, tips or pointers in their journeys to healing which you can utilize?
- Reflect on ways trauma can be destructive and yet promote self-growth.
- What qualities impede your progress to recovery?
- What qualities would you like to transform?
- What new behaviors do you need to learn?
- How can you integrate past behaviors and thoughts with the new ones you need to move forward and embrace the future?

EXERCISE

On a scale to 1 to 5, with 5 as the highest level, rate yourself in the follow areas.

RATING

Feeling **PURPOSEFUL** (i.e., engaging   _____
in goal-directed behavior)

Ability to maintain **FAITH**   _____

Feeling life is **MEANINGFUL** (i.e., Life has   _____
emotional or motivational significance to you)

Ability to maintain **HOPE**   _____

Heightened sense of **SPIRITUALITY** (i.e.,   _____
the belief in a higher power)

Ability to consistently practice **EVERYDAY**   _____
SACREDNESS

For ratings **3** or higher, **KEEP IT UP!!!!**

For any rating lower than **3**, select one area upon which to focus daily energy until your rating improve. Then, move on to the next area and focus energy there until your rating improves. Continue for other ratings below **3** until all your ratings are **3** or higher.

LIVE LIFE EACH MOMENT!

Chapter 12

Recovery versus Cure

As Steff and Alyce reminded us earlier, dealing with trauma is not a time-limited endeavor, but an ongoing process. If as a survivor you utilize those tools that best help you to cope, the adverse effects of traumatic events become less difficult to manage over time. Yes, there will still be occasions when you are broadsided by flashbacks and distressing moments. This is normal. However, through perseverance, you as a trauma survivor will be better equipped with tools to manage these periods. If you can view the skills you develop during the recovery process not as cure-alls but rather as tools to assist you in healing and coping with trauma's darker sides, you will move forward. Those individuals we've talked about in these pages have utilized such tools on their own journey of healing; so too can you. In this regard, your reflections on the lessons you have learned from your ordeal are indispensable.

Many of the survivors I've counseled learned lessons of the heart about those things that are of truest value to them. They have learned to communicate feeling and express their kindness, love, gratitude and spirituality. Some have learned that they could be scared and still go on with life. Others have learned valuable lessons about their inner strengths, hardiness and resilience. Still others have learned how to better face other challenges in their lives. These survivors have spoken of feeling more fortified, in general, after coping with their traumas. Many have told of being clearer about who they

are and what they want out of their lives. Other survivors have
learned that each day is a gift and that every human being is truly
unique and special in his or her own way.

As for me, there are many personal and professional lessons
that I have learned. In my private life I have learned how not to live
in terror; many other survivors with whom I've worked have found
the courage to do the same. I have learned not to allow a traumatic
event to diminish the quality of my life. I am learning to live my life
in this new reality. I've monitored my own responses to trauma and
been a witness to the reactions of others. I have renewed my own
being in ways I believe would not have occurred if not for the event.
I now live life on its own terms. That has freed me to enjoy not only
larger components but also the small joys of life, like watching the
leaves of autumn change colors. I have learned to be more attuned to
the setting sun, birds flying in formation and the rising moon.

I feel more comfortable and satisfied with whom I am now,
rather than obsessing about what I want to accomplish later. I no
longer concern myself with what before seemed so critical, but now,
in its proper perspective, is reduced to its rightful place. I have slowed
down, shortened my "to do" list and added to my "to be" list. I have
learned to eliminate the fear of silence. Instead, I now take in the inner
peace that silence offers and use silence to integrate my experiences,
both personal and professional, in order to create opportunity out of
crisis. I feel freer and, oddly enough, am now living my life more fear-
lessly.

In my professional life I have been shown first-hand how
trauma takes on infinite manifestations and paths and that recovery
from trauma does not flow in a straight line with phases that are
clearly demarcated. I have learned that each individual is capable of
courage and heroic acts.

I have learned to value different approaches to recovery. I
have discovered that for some, drawing strongly on their own internal resources works. For others it may be religious beliefs; for some,
family, friends and other support systems are most likely to help them
recover. I have also learned that, for still others to heal and recover
from trauma, assistance from professionals who can teach them tools
for coping is essential. I have learned that for some, the best approach
to healing is a combination of psychotherapy and medication; for others behavior modification works best. I found that there are various

psychological treatments successfully used for different individuals with varied backgrounds, beliefs, and personality traits.

For those survivors requiring in-depth treatment, cognitive-behavioral treatments, which generally offer a diverse number of methods including anxiety management, desensitization and cognitive restructuring techniques to minimize, for example, newly formed catastrophic beliefs following a disaster, have been very successful. For others, EMDR treatments are effective. EMDR attempts to mitigate trauma's potentially long-term effects and generally includes a combination of techniques (in particular, the use of rhythmic stimulation and eye movement) with the aim of assisting the survivor to re-process and integrate the traumatic event. Still others benefit from combinations of these two techniques with other psychological treatments. Fundamentally, I know conclusively now that "one size does not fit all" and that the healing journey of each survivor must be approached from his or her own unique perspectives, culture, values and personality traits.

While one size does not fit all, in my professional experience, with all things being equal, single or heterogeneous group sessions are not adequate alone in assisting survivors who suffer serious symptoms of post-traumatic stress syndrome to sustained healing and recovery. I have found that such sessions, in the early days after trauma are too distressing for some and for others, offer too little. "Psychological first aid," or providing early emotional ventilation and access to other support and social mechanisms, appears to be of more value to survivors of many types of trauma.

When I assess my own traumatic experience and my work with other survivors, as well as World Trade Center survivors, against my professional doctrines, I have found some of my earlier theories and beliefs changed. It was previously assumed that close proximity to the event and a feeling of surreality during the event would be significant indicators for chronic symptoms or post-traumatic stress disorder.

However, I have found that, in general, a large number of survivors of 9/11 had senses of surreality during their experiences and therefore this kind of reaction was not indicative of chronic difficulties in emotional, psychological, social, occupational and behavioral functioning. I also found that proximity was not indicative of functional impairment, as those who repeatedly witnessed the event on television and in the comfort of their homes (some were hundreds of miles away from the site) also experienced serious post-traumatic reactions like those who were directly affected.

In connection with the September 11th trauma, it was also not borne out that people who had prior psychiatric histories were the first to come for outside help. For instance, the first two hundred survivors with whom I met were by and large individuals with no prior psychiatric history. In addition, many articulate and high-functioning people with excellent coping skills prior to the traumatic event had sudden severe impairments in functioning, such as the inability to work, the development of stuttering symptoms that impaired their ability to function and marital discord. Finally, a notable percentage of individuals experienced delayed reactions and many felt more distressed on the second year anniversary of the event and thereafter.

Overall, I have found general interventions more helpful to survivors of many types of trauma including violent crimes, natural disasters and suicide, as well as others. For instance, following the immediate aftermath of trauma, early interventions that appeared most helpful to survivors have included: the solidification of support system delivery; the strengthening of personal resources and attention to the alleviation of anxiety and hyper-arousal states. As survivors I have known and worked with have moved toward integration of their traumas, the development of "new normal," desensitization procedures, managing continuing symptoms and attending to the enhancement of personal assets have been the factors that were most likely to result in positive recovery outcomes.

In my own work with survivors of trauma, I have found that offering each survivor empathic initial contact, practical and emotional support and treating each individual uniquely through proper screening and assessment, as well as individualized interventions, are the most successful ways to aid trauma sufferers to recover and heal.

Chapter 12 Resilience Tips

- List your "recipe" for successfully coping with your trauma.
- Reflect on the previously hidden opportunities that your trauma may have subsequently revealed to you.
- Reflect on ways in which you feel you have grown during your process of healing and recovery.
- What changes have you made, in your inner and outer life?
- What changes do you want to make?
- Write down how your perspective has evolved.
- Write down "lessons learned" from your experience.
- Reflect on your insights into yourself before, during and after the trauma.
- Reflect on how your feelings about those close to you have changed.
- Reflect on your new insights and perspectives about life and the future.

Chapter 13

Life's Healing Powers:
Everyday Sacredness

After successfully coping with trauma, survivors often find that lying before them are many other paths, each leading to a greater understanding of purpose and meaning in their lives. At this point many survivors look beyond the concrete ramifications of their traumas and ask themselves, *What was the purpose of experiencing this trauma? What was this event trying to teach me?*

Deriving purpose and meaning from a traumatic event is not an easy task, yet it can be a fulfilling accomplishment. The act of looking beyond the hardship created by trauma in search of a greater understanding of purpose and meaning has led numerous survivors to a hidden cache of riches. Such survivors' views of themselves and the world around them have been transformed. As I talk to them, they express feelings of energy and enthusiasm for life and the new horizons they had found both inside and outside themselves.

While Bob, one such survivor, continued to endure bouts of pain as an outcome of his traumatic injury, he rarely spoke of his physical anguish. Instead, he talked about his newfound appreciation for all things in his life—from each breath he takes to being given one more day to celebrate the myriad sights and sounds of the world. He has found meaning and purpose when he stopped being the workaholic businessman he thought he had to be in order to succeed. Instead, he has become the best father, husband and friend he can be. "Yes, I still work and enjoy my job even more now," Bob told me. "But work does not define me anymore. When I integrated the trauma I'd suffered, I opened my eyes fully and looked around. It was then I realized that my purpose was to make a positive contribution by sharing all parts of me with those I love. Once the blinders were off, I found true meaning in my life."

Like Bob, after acknowledging and accepting her trauma, Janet found new purpose and meaning in her life. Having finally worked through the aftermath of her traumatic experience, she talks of possessing an unbounded joy. "When I wake in the morning I almost feel like a child on Christmas morning. I feel gleeful in anticipation of the day ahead. Though I will never forget my trauma, I truly believe I finally opened my eyes to the singing of birds or the enjoyable antics of a toddler and all of the positive energy around me. I came to the realization that my purpose in life is to share that joy with others."

In his pilgrimage of recovery, Patrick was also led to a renewed sense of purpose and meaning. As he healed emotionally from the death of his friend in a fatal machinery accident, he allowed himself to acknowledge that life goes on despite tragedy. As he looked within, Patrick began to feel a burning desire to do something about other workplace tragedies. Patrick enrolled in safety training courses and began to teach industrial employees how to be safe in the workplace. In this way, Patrick created new meaning in his life.

Another triumphant survivor with whom I worked, Carol, let go of self-sabotaging beliefs and behaviors, allowing room in her life to cultivate her creative purpose. After following through on her educational goals, Carol used her artistic abilities to help other child abuse victims give expression to their trauma. This endeavor provided purpose and meaning to her life.

As Helen came to grips with the aftermath of her trauma, she felt an ever-increasing need to paint—a pleasurable activity she had set aside years before. Heeding the call to her artistic endeavors, she began to feel more and more calm and at peace with herself. Helen's relationship with her children improved dramatically, her job no longer felt burdensome and she smiled and appreciated life more.

What the successes of these personal journeys illustrate is a capacity that we are all blessed with: the capacity to balance adversity with imagination, to create self-fulfilling mental visions of our recovery. However, imagining recovery during periods of despair can be as obscure as trauma is stark. Such a mental picture of recovery requires seeing beyond the glare of trauma, visualizing the possibilities of healing and the purpose and meaning that lie ahead. In essence, faith and hope must reside with visions of recovery.

Hope and faith in one's ability to conquer major life challenges are the building blocks upon which the human spirit can be regenerated. And while all traumatic events assail the survivor's psyche, the tenacity of the human spirit can never be underestimated. After trauma, that spirit may reveal itself merely as a wish to seek healing and recovery. This, however, is the beginning of forward motion in seeking a better life or peace in the world. Tenacity of spirit drives us all to live life to its fullest. And once we call upon it to help us through adversity, we acknowledge its healing potential.

I have found that those survivors who embrace adversity's wisdom find in their battered but resilient spirit the strength to weather the storms of fear, grief, sorrow and despair they lived through. Once they had passed through the storm, their spirits assumed new forms and offered them the opportunities to strengthen, deepen, develop, rediscover or newly create purpose and meaning in their lives. This, in essence, is the healing journey.

In times of trauma and its aftermath, faith and hope may seem elusive assets that rely primarily on intangibles, non-material qualities we can neither feel or touch. We often apply terms like "working through" and "processing" to these dynamics that often defy description. However, as these two elements regenerate in the lives of survivors, whether they are aided by remaining loved ones, introspection, professional counseling or a combination of these aids, they are crucial in the pilgrimage to healing.

Sometimes, contrary to the evidence, faith and hope enjoin us to trust that the solution to our wishes, desires and needs will materialize in some shape or form. For some of us, however, this is a threatening quandary, for faith and hope were easier to clasp when we were children and believed without limits of rationality and reality the myths of tooth fairies, Easter bunnies and Santa Claus.

When we are young adults, feeling immortal, the power of faith and hope seems at our fingertips. However, once confronted by terrible realities, many feel, at least at first, they must rely on ego and rational self to move onward through life.

Trauma survivors learn that their egos or rational selves are often not enough to transcend their ordeals. In fact, the ego often becomes stuck in such states as denial, anxiety, guilt and despair. It is the ego that tells us, "No, my tragedy didn't really happen." It is the ego that says we should be anxious. The ego demands that we should feel guilty. The ego leads us to despair. Yet I have seen that both faith and hope are important. Faith in the belief that we can and we will heal from our trauma seems to be a necessary element for healing to occur. Hope that life will be better in the future appears to be central to recovery. The many survivors with whom I have worked have showed me that when faced with adversity, faith and hope can be rediscovered by people and used generously to help them along their healing paths.

Survivors who hold on to or find renewed faith and hope as they journey onward are especially blessed. These survivors are able to take their healing journeys to the next level and thus find themselves with an abundance of life-giving gifts. They seem to radiate with the wisdom we all secretly crave and through their radiance generously bestow upon us gifts of fulfillment and contentment.

Many survivors also cease to view adversity as "bad luck," but rather perceive it as a challenge and opportunity to learn something new about themselves and others. I believe that reaching this critical juncture in their journey, they approach challenges from the perspective of students and picture life as a classroom. At this point they are able to face their challenges with focused energy. Even though in the beginning many ask, "Why me?" I have heard many say as they heal, "Why not me?" and "I'm ready." However, since in their journey most survivors have bad times as well as good, during those times when they feel that they might be losing ground, they look attentively around themselves to find hope and faith. The two again provide them with the courage to move forward.

Though earlier in their lives some survivors haven't thought a lot about the meaning of life or death, after trauma, issues of faith, hope, meaning and purpose seem to invoke questions and ideas for many about "spirituality" or the belief in a power higher than oneself. Some survivors had rigid theories, then begin to wonder what if any of these still apply and then reconstruct their beliefs, adopting a broader view of the elements of spirituality. Talking to survivors I have learned that while spirituality comes in many forms and invokes many names, all forms of spirituality seem to rely on the recognition and acceptance of a higher power, one that offers inspiration.

However, I have also found in my work with trauma survivors that spirituality takes on many configurations, from deriving inspiration as one gazes out upon the ocean to finding the uniqueness inherent in every individual. I have sat with many survivors who have achieved in their healing journeys higher levels of spirituality than they ever thought they could reach when mired in despair, depression, grief, gloom and sadness.

Reflecting, it seems that spirituality by way of trauma can transform one's entire being. Survivors tell of dramatic shifts in their attitudes about themselves and the world around them. They speak of feeling more empathic and tolerant and of letting go of self and other limiting notions. Many exhibit senses of great peace of mind and calm and some indicate through their manner that they now accept reality in whatever form it comes their way. It seems that it would take a special kind of person to transcend trauma in this way. Yet, I have seen "ordinary" people harness life's healing powers and do it over and over again. What ultimately emerges is that such survivors strengthen their capacities to give and receive unconditional love. The individual appears to have come full circle—to the recognition, acknowledgement and appreciation of the ordinary.

Everyday Sacredness

Survivors are often startled by the realization that the key to their healing is most often discovered within new appreciation of the ordinary. They have come to know that learning to acknowledge the value of moments of normalcy in everyday life, instead of the trauma of adversity, rejuvenates them. Most conclude that healing finally comes when they accept and embrace each moment. I believe these survivors have learned one of the greatest lessons in life—the sacredness of every day.

Survivors who practice what I call "everyday sacredness" do so in unique and singular ways, each from their own perspective. I have found that some practice it through meditation, while others do so by traveling to far-away places so that they may gaze upon beautiful vistas. Still others practice everyday sacredness by doing photography or journal writing. Some individuals practice it through prayer or with affirmations. Still others find everyday sacredness in those moments when they gaze at family members with loving eyes or when they sit on a park bench, observing and appreciating the uniqueness of all who pass by.

All of these expressions of everyday sacredness can be defined as the acknowledgment, acceptance and quiet rejoicing in what is before us. The practice of everyday sacredness is, I believe, without judgment, insecurities, anxiety, fear or expectation. It is simply the ability to fully appreciate life on its own terms and find the beauty of life in the here and now. Each survivor finds his own definition. It is as simple as watching a red robin as it sits atop a telephone pole and saying a silent "happy adventure" as it flies away to the next perch. It can be as easy as seeing a friendly face and smiling in return. It can be as effortless as gazing over at your spouse or best friend and thinking, *Now here is a really good person.*

Survivors of trauma who have healed seem in many ways primed to discover everyday sacredness. This is not to say that survivors are lucky to have had traumatic experiences, but rather living through abnormal incidents seems to propel people to appreciate everything in their lives.

Antoinette spoke of wearing clothes that she had been saving for a "special day," realizing that "every day is special." Janet shared with me that every day feels like a holiday, while Steff related that he no longer puts off for tomorrow what he can do today.

In a global sense, trauma can also compel us to work against chronic negative states that preceded our trauma such as melancholy, malaise, boredom or a feeling of incompleteness. Trauma, by its nature, forces us away from characteristic behaviors. Therefore it can be a catalyst in pushing us out of such states, even if only temporarily. Indeed, some survivors found that in their earlier lives they were struggling to overcome chronic negative states and in recovery are now acting to address these characteristics in their lives.

Numerous times during his struggle to feel loved and cared for, life presented one survivor of trauma, Nick, with everyday lessons about its healing power. During his childhood, Nick's eldest brother tried to teach him about the healing power of everyday life and during his adolescence, numerous schoolteachers attempted to teach him this lesson. When Nick enlisted in the army, this new course in his life also presented him with an opportunity to master this lesson. In some unconscious way, Nick himself was indicating that he was ready to learn. However, it took the trauma of war, subsequent post-traumatic stress, depression and rage to force him to pay full attention in the classroom of life. Nick then paused, took notes and began to unburden himself of that which ailed him, finally allowing everyday life to heal him.

At forty-one years old, Nick has found meaning and purpose in his life and now practices everyday sacredness. He works diligently at being the best husband to his wife, the best father to his four-year-old son and the best ally to his friends. He now believes that his purpose in life is to love fully and unconditionally. Nick often speaks of intimacy and relation to others, states that had evaded him for many years. He now relies on faith and hope to get him through difficulties and trusts that there must be another lesson to be learned from them.

For many years Mara struggled with anxieties and fears, such as fear of driving and panic in large crowds, that negatively impacted many areas of her life. Yet it was only following a traumatic event that Mara began to face situations she had avoided most of her life. She expressed interest in learning to drive; she willingly exposed herself to large crowds and began to imagine a more fulfilling life.

Nick, Mara and other survivors I have known have been able to successfully stand up to adversity and as they progressed on their journeys have called upon and strengthened themselves spiritually. These individuals now use the spirit that lives in all of us as a healing tonic and drink it daily. They have, in effect, opened themselves up to themselves and others in immeasurable ways. These survivors have faith and hope and greater senses of self and meaning in their reconstituted lives. They report feeling senses of "wholeness" and fulfillment, the antithesis of melancholy, boredom or uneasiness. In recovering, these survivors have embraced the healing power of life by opening themselves up to and recognizing the everyday sacredness of life.

At the beginning of my own traumatic experience's aftermath, I noted that the process of recovery felt like a pendulum forcing me to one extreme in order to swing back to a normal alignment. Perhaps it is out of that process that the potential for everyday sacredness emerges. While the momentum may be initially propelled by fear or despair, perhaps as the pendulum reaches the limit of its arc, it sheds much of the fear or despair and a regrouping of the true essentials of life becomes possible. For me, the pendulum swung to its opposite pole and then settled down to a new normal. This process changed me in many positive ways. It forced me to be in the moment, both emotionally and spiritually. Like many others, my trauma has taught me that every day is sacred, never to be taken for granted. It has confirmed for me that which has always been in my nature—to make positive connections with those I encounter and to share my knowledge and skills so that others may benefit.

One of my clients, Sharon, came to appreciate everyday sacredness from another route. As she reintegrated her trauma and resumed those things that she had been avoiding, such as driving and re-bonding with her husband, she began to enjoy her life more and more. As this process unfolded, her sights shifted from enjoying the day to reveling in the moment. She began to live in the moment and found contentment there. She shared these reflections with me: "When I am in the moment, life then seems infinite. There is so much to see and hear in each moment—trees, the sky, city noise, grass and chirping birds. The beauty of a moment goes on and on."

Painting the wooden molding around a window, arranging flowers in a vase or hanging a picture in your home are a few of the countless number of ways of practicing everyday sacredness. Doing such tasks and pausing to reflect on the beauty of the ordinary bring outs the richness and vitality of life. Many survivors with whom I've talked feel that in practicing everyday sacredness they have been nourished by life's beauty and are therefore more capable of dealing with life's challenges. From the witness of their successful experience to their passages into recovery, survivors invite us all not to forget the future but to embrace everyday sacredness, to live and appreciate the moment.

Conclusion

I hope all who are coping with agony, sorrow, pain and anger due to traumatic experiences have been comforted by the survivors' stories highlighted in this book. They have shared their traumas, the aftermaths and the repercussions that can occur in dealing with tragic experiences' darker elements. They have allowed you to bear witness to their grief and pain because they care. For this reason they have offered you, who also may be suffering, the opportunity to walk with them as they took their first tentative steps on healing paths and have invited you to accompany them on their journeys. They have shared their sorrows and joys with you as they healed and regained or created balance in their new lives. They have revealed to you that though crisis unearths pain, it can also unmask opportunity. They have shared with you the ways in which new opportunities came. They have given freely of themselves in order to inspire resilience, healing and self-discovery in you who are also facing trauma in your lives.

As a survivor myself, I feel their personal healing journeys are poignant examples of courage from which those who have lived through trauma may draw inspiration. They demonstrate that healing takes on many forms and permutations so that all individuals may feel free to heal in their own unique ways. Like those in this book who persevered on their individual healing paths, just as they emerged forever changed in their essence, you too, I believe, can walk down healing roads. They emerged stronger and resilient, experienced yet innocent in front of life's wonders, wiser, yet humbled by the beauty of each moment. I wish this for you as well.

These survivors are both ordinary and extraordinary. In many ways they display all our commonalities. They struggled, faltered and resisted the inevitable change tragedy brought as we all do. Their wishes, hopes, desires and needs are similar to the wishes, hopes, desires and needs we all share. Yet they have also moved forward on extraordinary journeys. On healing paths they learned to accept life on its own terms and manage what is manageable. They sustained emotional pain and found their way through storms of despair. They searched and found something greater than their trauma. And, as they recovered, they found the courage to reach out to life and embrace it. In this way, they show us all that we too can accept and conquer the challenges of life.

Like these individuals, I hope you can gain the strength and fortitude to seek the lessons hidden in trauma and to call on your spirit to help you cope, just as they learned to seek, nurture and cultivate the many positive parts of themselves and to share those parts with families and friends. You too can live again. The survivors' stories in this book demonstrate that in so doing we are, in essence, allowing the beauty of our spirits to expand outward and beyond ourselves, into the world. Through their struggles and healing processes, these survivors show the way, after trauma humbles and hurts us, to discover the beauty in everyday life, to appreciate the moment and to give freely of unique gifts.

These survivors show us that there are new heights of self-awareness we still can reach after trauma changes and impacts our lives and that we all have the ability to soar beyond our own expectations. They teach us that out of crisis, opportunity may rise and provide us with daily lives that, although different, are filled with infinite riches. The heart of the matter is that these survivors can teach us how to begin again. They show us how trauma goes through various stages with many manifestations which may cause pain at any juncture.

Once committed to healing paths, we can begin to refashion our lives. Knowing that others have walked on dark, difficult roads and reached destinations of light will, I hope, be comforting. The realization that many survivors have recovered to find purpose and meaning will, I hope, give you hope. For from their trauma survivors' healing journeys, we can discover that trauma's saving grace is that it is not irrevocable but ultimately surmountable and enriching. You too can learn to live again.

Resilience Tips

- Practice focused observation daily.
- Close your eyes, clear your mind and sit quietly for five minutes. Then look around you. What do you see? What do you feel?
- Reflect on if and how your trauma has given you renewed purpose and meaning in your life.
- When you have healed, give your spirit a joyful name and call on it whenever you feel the need.
- Believe in and plan for your future, but live for and savor each day.

References

General:

Arcangel, Dianne and Raymond A. Moody Jr. *Life After Loss: Conquering Grief and Finding Hope.* Harper San Francisco, 2001.

Bozarth, Alla Renee. *A Journey through Grief: Gentle, Specific Help to Get You Through the Most Difficult Stages of Grieving.* Hazelden Publishing and Educational Services, 1990.

Canfield, Jack and Mark Hansen. *Chicken Soup for the Grieving Soul: Stories About Life, Death and Overcoming the Loss of a Loved One.* Health Communications, 2003.

Caplan, Sandi and Gordon Lang. *Grief's Courageous Journey: A Workbook.* New Harbinger Publications: Oakland, CA, 1995.

Ericsson, Stephanie. *Companion Through the Darkness: Inner Dialogues on Grief.* Perennial, 1993.

Fitzgerald, Helen. *The Mourning Handbook: The Most Comprehensive Resource Offering Practical and Compassionate Advice on Coping with All Aspects of Death and Dying.* Simon and Schuster, 1995.

Hickman, Martha. Healing *After Loss: Daily Meditations for Working Through Grief.* Avon, 1999.

James, John W. and Russell Friedman. *Grief Recovery Handbook - the Action Program For Moving Beyond Death, Divorce, and Other Losses.* Harper Collins, 1998.

Kubler-Ross, Elisabeth. *Death, the Final Growth Stage.* Simon and Schuster, 1997.

—*On Death and Dying.* Simon and Schuster, 1997.

—*Living with Death and Dying.* Simon and Schuster, 1997.

—*Questions and Answers on Death and Dying.* Simon and Schuster, 1997.

—*Death.* Touchstone Books, 1997.

Levang, Elizabeth. *Remembering with Love: Messages of Hope for the First Year of Grieving and Beyond.* Deaconess Press, 1992.

Lewis, C.S. *A Grief Observed.* Bantam Doubleday Dell: New York, 1976.

Lord, Janice H. *No Time for Goodbyes: Coping with Sorrow, Anger and Injustice After a Tragic Death.* Pathfinder Publishing of California, 1991.

Mayo, Peg E. *The Healing Sorrow Workbook: Rituals for Transforming Grief and Loss.* New Harbinger Publications, 2001.

Mitsch, Ray and Lynn Brookside. *Grieving the Loss of Someone You Love: Daily Meditations to Help You Through the Grieving Process.* Vine Books, 1993.

Noel, Brook and Pamela D. Blair. *I Wasn't Ready to Say Goodbye: Surviving, Coping and Healing after the Death of a Loved One.* Champion Press, Limited, 2000.

Prend, Ashley Davis. *Transcending Loss: Understanding the Lifelong Impact of Grief and How to Make It Meaningful*. Berkeley Publishing Group, 1997.

Rando, Therese A. *How to Go on Living when Someone You Love Dies*. Bantam Doubleday Dell, 1991.

Rinpoche, Sogyal. *The Tibetan Book of Living and Dying*. Harper: San Francisco, 2002.

Russell, Sherry. *Conquering the Mysteries and Lies of Grief*. PublishAmerica Inc., 2002.

Schweibert, Pat and Chuck DeKlyen. *Tear Soup*. Perinatal Loss, 2001.

Staudacher, Carol. *A Time to Grieve: Meditations for Healing After the Death of a Loved One*. Harper San Francisco, 1994.

Tatelbaum, Judy. *The Courage to Grieve*. Perennial, 1984.

Temes, Roberta. *Living with an Empty Chair: A Guide Through Grief*. New Horizon Press: Far Hills, 1992.

Van Praagh, James. *Healing Grief: Reclaiming Life After Any Loss*. E P Dutton, 2000.

Walton, Charlie. *When There Are No Words: Finding Your Way to Cope With Loss and Grief*. Pathfinder Publishing of California, 1996.

Westberg, Granger E.. *Good Grief: A Constructive Approach to the Problem of Loss*. Augsburg Fortress, 1983.

Wolfelt, Alan. *Healing Your Traumatized Heart: 100 Practical Ideas After Someone You Love Dies a Sudden, Violent Death* (Healing Your Grieving Heart Series). Companion Press, 2002.

Death of a Child:

Bernstein, Judith. *When the Bough Breaks: Forever After the Death of a Son or Daughter*. Andrews McMeel Publishing, 1998.

Bolton, Iris and Curtis Mitchell. *My Son...My Son: A Guide to Healing After Death, Loss, or Suicide*. Bolton Press: Atlanta, 1983.

Finkbeiner, Ann K. *After the Death of a Child: Living With Loss Through the Years*. Johns Hopkins University Press, 1998.

Kubler-Ross, Elizabeth. *On Children and Death*. Simon and Schuster, 1997.
McCracken, Anne and Mary Semel. *A Broken Heart Still Beats: After Your Child Dies*. Hazelden Information Education, 2000.

Mehren, Elizabeth. *After the Darkest Hour the Sun Will Shine Again: A Parent's Guide to Coping with the Loss of a Child*. Fireside, 1997.

Rosof, Barbara. *The Worst Loss: How Families Heal from the Death of a Child*. Henry Hold and Company, Inc., 1995.

Sander, Catherine M. *How to Survive the Loss of a Child: Filling the Emptiness and Rebuilding Your Life*. Prima Lifestyles, 1998.

Schiff, Harriet Sarnoff. *The Bereaved Parent*. Viking Press: New York, 1978.

Strommen, Merton. *Five Cries of Grief: One Family's Journey to Healing After the Tragic Death of a Son*. Augsburg Fortress Publishers, 1996.

Wiersbe, David. *Gone but Not Lost: Grieving the Death of a Child*. Baker Book House, 1992.

Wolterstorff, Nicholas. *Lament for a Son*. William B. Eerdmans Publishing Co., 1987.

Loss of Infant Child:

Davis, Deborah L. *Empty Cradle, Broken Heart: Surviving the Death of Your Baby*. Fulcrum Publishers: Golden, CO, 1996.

Eddy, Mary L. and Linda Raydo. *Making Loving Memories: A Gentle Guide to What You Can Do When Your Baby Dies*. Centering Corporation, 1990.

Goodman, Sandy. *Love Never Dies: A Mother's Journey From Loss to Love*. Jodere Group, 2002.

Ikenberry, Christine K. Heaven's *Child: Recovering from the Loss of an Infant*. iUniverse.com, 2003.

Kohn, Ingrid, et al. *A Silent Sorrow: Pregnancy Loss-Guidance and Support for You and Your Family*. Routledge, 2000.

Lafser, Christine O'Keefe and Phyllis Tickle. *An Empty Cradle, a Full Heart: Reflections for Mothers and Fathers After Miscarriage, Stillbirth or Infant Death*. Loyola Press, 1998.

Limbo, Rana K. *When a Baby Dies: A Handbook for Healing and Helping*. Bereavement Services, 1987.

Lothrop, Hannah. *Help, Comfort and Hope After Losing Your Baby in Pregnancy or the First Year*. Perseus Publishing, 1997.

Wittwer, Sherri Devashrayee. *Gone Too Soon: The Life and Loss of Infants and Unborn Children*. Covenant Communications, 1994.

Death of a Spouse:

Anthony, Nancy. *Mourning Thoughts: Facing a New Day After the Death of a Spouse*. Twenty-third Publications, 1991.

Brumett, Grace, et al., ed. *When a Lifemate Dies: Stories of Love, Loss and Healing*. Fairview Press, 1997.

Caine, Lynn. *Being a Widow*. Penguin USA: New York, 1990.

Colgrove, Melba, et al. *How to Survive the Loss of a Love*. Prelude Press, 1993.

Feinberg, Linda Sones. *I'm Grieving as Fast as I Can: How Young Widows and Widowers Can Cope and Heal*. New Horizon Press: Far Hills, 1994.

Felber, Marta. *Finding Your Way After Your Spouse Dies*. Ave Maria Press, 2000.
—*Grief Expressed: When a Mate Dies*. Fairview Press, 2002.

Ginsburg, Genevieve Davis. *Widow to Widow: Thoughtful, Practical Ideas for Rebuilding Your Life*. Perseus Publishing, 1999.

Lund, Dale A. ed. <u>Older</u> *Bereaved Spouses: Research with Practical Applications* (Series in Death Education Aging and Health Care. Hemisphere, 1989.

Young, Kathy and Gary Young. *Loss and Found: How We Survived the Loss of a Young Spouse*. Calabash Press, 2001.

Zonnebelt-Smeenge, Susan J. and Robert C. De Vries. *Getting to the Other Side of Grief: Overcoming the Loss of a Spouse*. Baker Books, 1998.

Death of a Parent:

Bartocci, Barbara. *Nobody's Child Anymore: Grieving, Caring, and Comforting When Parents Die*. Sorin Books, 2000.

Brooks, Jane. *Midlife Orphan: Facing Life's Changes Now That Your Parents Are Gone*. Berkeley Publishing Group, 1999.

Chatman, Delle. *The Death of Parent: Reflections for Adults Mourning the Loss of a Father or Mother*. ACTA Publications, 2003.

Chethik, Neil. *FatherLoss: How Sons of All Ages Come to Terms with the Deaths of their Dads*. Hyperion, 2001.

Edelman, Hope. *Motherless Daughters: The Legacy of Loss*. Delta, 1995.

Erickson, Beth. *Looking for Dad: Father Loss and Its Impact*. Health Communications, 1998.

Gilbert, Richard. *Finding Your Way After Your Parent Dies*. Ave Maria Press, 1999.

Harris, Maxine. *The Loss That Is Forever: The Lifelong Impact of the Early Death of a Mother or Father*. Plume, 1996.

Kennedy, Alexandra. *Losing a Parent: Passage to a New Way of Living*. Harper San Francisco, 2001.

Levy, Alexander. *The Orphaned Adult: Understanding and Coping with Grief and Change After the Death of Our Parents*. Perseus Publishing, 2001.

Marshall, Fiona. *Losing a Parent: Practical Help for You and Other Family Members*. Perseus Publishing, 2000.

Myers, Edward. *When Parents Die: A Guide for Adults*. Penguin USA: New York, 1987.

Secunda, Victoria. *Losing Your Parents Finding Yourself: The Defining Turning Point of Adult Life*. Hyperion, 2001.

Simon, Clea. <u>Fatherless </u>Women: How We Change After We Lose Our Dads. John Wiley and Sons, 2002.

Simon, Leslie and Jan Johnson Drantell. A Music I No Longer Heard: The Early Death of a Parent. Simon and Schuster, 1998.

Smith, Harold Ivan. On Grieving the Death of a Father. Fortress Press, 1994.

Wakerman, Elyce. Father Loss: Daughters Discuss the Man that Got Away. Henry Holt and Company, Inc., 1987.

For Grieving Children and Teens:

Buscaglia, Leo F. *The Fall of Freddie the Leaf: 20th Anniversary Edition.* Henry Holt & Company, Inc., 2002.

Dougy Center. *35 Ways to Help a Grieving Child.* The Dougy Center for Grieving Children, 1999.

Dower, Laura. *I Will Remember You: What to Do When Someone You Love Dies: A Guidebook Through Grief for Teens.* Harper Collins, 2001.

Emswiller, Mary Ann and James P. Emswiller. *Guiding Your Child Through Grief.* Bantam Books, 2000.

Fitzgerald, Helen. *The Grieving Child.* Fireside, 1992.

Grollman, Earl A. *Straight Talk About Death for Teenagers: How to Cope with Losing Someone You Love.* Beacon Press, 1993.

—*Talking About Death: A Dialogue Between Parent and Child.* Beacon Press, 1991.

Heegaard, Marge. *When Someone Very Special Dies: Children Can Learn to Cope with Grief.* Woodland Press: Minneapolis, MN, 1988.

—*When Something Terrible Happens: Children Can Learn to Cope with Grief.* Woodland Press: Minneapolis, MN, 1992.

Krasny, Laurie and Marc Brown. *When Dinosaurs Die: Guide to Understanding Death.* Little Brown and Company, 1996.

Krementz, Jill. *How It Feels When a Parent Dies.* Knopf: New York, 1998.

Kroen, William C. *Helping Children Cope With the Loss of a Loved One: A Guide for Grownups.* Free Spirit Publishing, 1996.

Mellonie, Bryan. *Lifetimes: The Beautiful Way to Explain Death to Children.* Bantam Books: New York, 1983.

Mundy, Michaelene. *Sad Isn't Bad: A Good-Grief Guidebook for Kids Dealing with Loss*. Abbey Press, 1998.

Romain, Trevor. *What on Earth Do You Do When Someone Dies?*. Free Spirit Publishing, 1999.

Shriver, Maria. *What's Heaven?* Golden Books Adult Publishing, 1999.

Silverman, Janis. *Help Me Say Goodbye: Activities for Helping Kids Cope When a Special Person Dies*. Fairview Press, 1999.

Temes, Roberta. *The Empty Place: A Child's Guide Through Grief*. New Horizon Press: Far Hills, NJ, 1992.

Traisman, Enid Samuel. *Fire in My Heart, Ice in My Veins: A Journal for Teenagers Experiencing Loss*. Centering Corporation, 1992.

Wolfelt, Alan D. *Healing a Child's Grieving Heart*. Companion Press, 2001.

Worden, J. William. *Children and Grief*. Guilford Press, 2001.

On Surviving Traumatic Situations:

Foley, Bob. *The Death of Innocence: Surviving Trauma.* 1st Books Library, 2002.

Lattanzi-Licht, Marcia. *Living with Grief: Coping with Public Tragedy.* Brunner-Routledge, 2003.

MacInnis, Joseph. *Surviving Terrorism: How to Protect Your Health, Wealth and Safety.* Deep Anchor Press, 2002.

Montgomery, Bob and Laurel Morris. *Surviving: Coping with a Life Crisis.* Perseus Publishing, 2000.

Slaby, Andrew E. Aftershock: *Surviving the Delayed Effects of Trauma, Crisis and Loss.* Random House: New York, 1989.

U.S. Department of Justice, Office of Justice Programs, Office for Victims of Crime. "Coping After Terrorism: A Guide to Healing and Recovery." <http://www.ojp.usdoj.gov/ovc/publications/infores/cat_hndbk/welcome.html>.

U.S. Marine Corps. *The Individual's Guide to Understanding and Surviving Terrorism.* Fredonia Books, 2002.

Losing a Loved One to Suicide:

Bolton, Iris and Curtis Mitchell. *My Son...My Son: A Guide to Healing After a Suicide in the Family*. Bolton Press Atlanta, 1983.

Burgess, Mary S. *Handbook of Hope: First Aid for Surviving the Suicide of a Loved One*. Sonbeam Press, 2000.

Fine, Carla. *No Time to Say Goodbye: Surviving the Suicide of a Loved One*. Main Street Books, 1999.

Hewett, John. *After Suicide*. Westminster Press: Louisville, KY, 1980.

Hsu, Albert. *Grieving a Suicide: A Loved One's Search for Comfort, Answers and Hope*. Intervarsity Press, 2002.

Jamison, Kay. *Night Falls Fast: Understanding Suicide*. Vintage Books, 2000.

Kolf, June. *Standing in the Shadow: Help and Encouragement for Suicide Survivors*. Baker Book House, 2002.

Miller, Sara Swan. *An Empty Chair: Living in the Wake of a Sibling's Suicide*. iUnvierse.com, 2000.

Ross, Eleanora B. *After Suicide: A Ray of Hope for Those Left Behind*. Perseus Publishing, 2002.

Robinson, Rita. *Survivors of Suicide*. Newcastle Publishing Co., 1992.

Scholz, Barb. Our *Forever Angel: Surviving the Loss of a Loved One to Suicide*. 1st Books Library, 2002.
Smolin, Ann. *Healing After the Suicide of a Loved One*. Fireside, 1993.

Wertheimer, Alison. *A Special Scar: The Experiences of People Bereaved by Suicide*. Brunner-Routledge, 2001.

Resources

Support organizations for those grieving the loss of a child:

Compassionate Friends
P.O. Box 3696
Oakbrook, IL 60522-3696
Phone: 630-990-0010
Fax: 630-990-0246
Toll Free: 877-969-0010
http://www.compassionatefriends.org/

Alive Alone
Kay Bevington, Alive Alone
11115 Dull Robinson Road
Van Wert, OH. 45891
Email: KayBevington@alivealone.org
http://www.alivealone.org/

Baby Steps
182-1054 Centre Street
Thornhill, ON
L4J 8E5, CANADA
Phone: 905-707-1030
Email: info@babysteps.com
http://www.babysteps.com/

Center for Grief Recovery/Institute for Creativity
1263 W. Loyola
Chicago, IL 60626
Phone: 773-274-4600
Email:CJRothman@Hotmail.com
http://www.griefcounselor.bigstep.com/

In Loving Memory
1416 Green Run Lane
Reston, VA 20190
Fax: (703) 435-3111
Email: InLvMemory@aol.com
http://www.inlovingmemoryonline.org/

Candlelighters Childhood Cancer Foundation
P.O. Box 498
Kensington MD 20895-0498
Phone: 301-962-3520
Fax: 301-962-3521
Toll-free: 800-366-CCCF
800-366-2223
Email: info@candlelighters.org
http://www.candlelighters.org/

Bereaved Parents of the USA
P.O. Box 95
Park Forest, Illinois 60466
Phone: 708-748-7672
Fax: 708-748-9184
http://www.bereavedparentsusa.org/

Pen-Parents, Inc.
P.O. Box 8738
Reno, Nevada 89507-8738
Phone: 702-322-4773
http://www.penparents.com

Center for Loss in Multiple Birth (CLIMB) Inc.
P.O. Box 91377
Anchorage AK 99509
Phone: 907-222-5321
Email: climb@pobox.alaska.net (Jean Kollantai)
http://www.climb-support.org/enabled/index.html

LARGO – Life After Repeated Grief Options
http://www.geocities.com/Heartland/Hills/9689/

MISS – Mothers in Sympathy and Support
Email: info@missfoundation.org
http://www.misschildren.org/

SHARE Pregnancy and Infant Loss Support, Inc.
National SHARE Office
St. Joseph Health Center
300 First Capitol Drive
St. Charles, Missouri 63301-2893
800-821-6819 or 636-947-6164
Fax: 636-947-7486
Email: share@nationalshareoffice.com
http://www.nationalshareoffice.com/

SIDS Alliance
1314 Bedford Avenue Suite 210
Baltimore, Maryland 21208
Phone: 800-221-SIDS
Fax: 410-653-8709
http://www.sidsalliance.org/index/default.asp

Association of SIDS and Infant Mortality Programs
http://www.asip1.org/

Feelings of the Fathers
http://www.thelaboroflove.com/forum/loss/fathers.html

Bereaved Single Mothers Forum
http://forums.delphiforums.com/bereavedsnglmom/start

MEND – Mommies Enduring Neonatal Death
http://www.mend.org/home_index.asp

UNITE
http://www.unite.freeservers.com/

SPALS – Subsequent Pregnancy After a Loss Support
http://www.spals.com/

A Heartbreaking Choice
http://www.erichad.com/

AGAST – Alliance of Grandparents, a Support in Tragedy
http://www.agast.org/

Support organizations for families of those killed:

National Organization for Victim Assistance (NOVA)
1730 Park Road NW
Washington DC 20010
Phone: 202-232-6682
Fax: 202-462-2255
http://www.try-nova.org/

Parents of Murdered Children
National POMC
100 East Eighth Street, Suite B-41
Cincinnati, Ohio 45202
Phone: 513-721-5683
Fax: 513-345-4489
Toll Free: 888-818-POMC
http://www.pomc.com
Email: natlpomc@aol.com

Tragedy Assistance Program for Survivors (TAPS) – Military Deaths
National Headquarters
2001 S Street, NW, Suite 300
Washington, DC 20009
Hotline: 800-959-TAPS(8277)
General Info: info@taps.org
Survivor Resources: help@taps.org
Volunteer Info: volunteer@taps.org
http://www.taps.org

Concerns of Police Survivors (COPS)
P.O. Box 3199
South Highway Five
Camdenton, MO 65020
Phone: 573-346-4911
Fax: 573-346-1414
Email: cops@nationalcops.org
http://www.nationalcops.org

Resources for Children:

The National Center for Grieving Children and Families
The Dougy Center
PO Box 86852
Portland OR 97286 USA
Phone: 503-775-5683
Fax: 503-777-3097
Email: help@dougy.org
http://www.dougy.org/

Fernside – A Center for Grieving Children
Bethesda Professional Building
4360 Cooper Road, Suite 101
Cincinnati, Ohio 45242
Phone: 513-745-0111
Fax: 513-745-0524
Email: info@fernside.org
http://www.fernside.org/

The Grieving Center for Children, Teens and Families
P. O. Box 57121
Philadelphia, PA   19111
Phone: 215-427-6767
Fax: 215-427-5971
Email: grievingchildren@aol.com
http://www.grievingchildren.org/

TAG – Teenage Grief
http://www.dansville.k12.ny.us/New%20Story/grief_counseling.htm

Loss of a Spouse:

Young Widows and Widowers
Phone: 845-463-2548
Email: lisawriter@msn.com
http://youngwidowsandwidowers.com/

Widownet:
http://www.fortnet.org/cgi-bin/ubb/ultimatebb.cgi

Young Widow:
http://www.youngwidow.com

Parents Without Partners
1650 South Dixie Highway, Suite 510
Boca Raton, FL 33432
Phone: 561-391-8833
Fax: 561-395-8557
Email: pwp@jti.net
http://www.parentswithoutpartners.org/

Loss of Sibling:

Adult Sibling Grief
http://www.adultsiblinggrief.com/

The Sibling Connection
http://www.counselingstlouis.net/index.html

Twinless Twins
http://www.twinlesstwins.org/

General:

Compassion Connection
http://www.compassionconnection.org/

Grief and Loss (AARP)
http://www.aarp.org/griefandloss/

GROWW – Grief and Bereavement Resources
http://www.groww.com/
Association for Death Education and Counseling
342 North Main Street
West Hartford, CT 06117-2507
Phone: 860-586-7503
Fax: 860-586-7550
Email: info@adec.org
http://www.adec.org

Center for Loss and Life Transition
3735 Broken Bow Road
Fort Collins, CO 80526
Phone: 970-226-6050
Fax: 970-226-6051
Email: wolfelt@centerforloss.com
http://www.centerforloss.com

Family Assistance Foundation – For survivors of and family members of those involved in airline accidents
1691 Phoenix Boulevard, Suite 150
Atlanta, Georgia 30349
Phone: 770-909-7474
Fax: 770-909-9552
Email: kate@fafonline.org
http://www.fafonline.org/

Grief, Loss and Recovery
http://www.grieflossrecovery.com/

Crisis, Grief and Healing
http://www.webhealing.com/

The Centering Corporation
http://www.centering.org/

Grief Watch
2116 NE 18th Ave
Portland, OR   97212
Phone: 503-284-7426
Fax: 503-282-8985
Email: webmaster@griefwatch.com
http://www.griefwatch.com/

Beyond Indigo
http://www.beyondindigo.com/

Grief Healing
http://www.griefhealing.com/

The Bright Side
http://www.the-bright-side.org/site/thebrightside/

Surviving Suicide:

Centre for Suicide Prevention
Suicide Information & Education Centre
1615 - 10th Avenue S.W. Suite 201
Calgary, Alberta T3C 0J7
Canada
Phone: 403-245-3900
http://www.suicideinfo.ca/

SOS – Survivors of Suicide
American Foundation for Suicide Prevention
120 Wall Street, 22nd Floor
New York, New York 10005
Phone: 212-363-3500
Fax: -212-363-6237
Toll-free: 888-333-AFSP
Email: inquiry@afsp.org
http://www.afsp.org/

American Association of Suicidology
4201 Connecticut Avenue, N.W.
Suite 310
Washington, D.C. 20008
Phone: 202-237-2280
http://www.suicidology.org/

National Catholic Ministry to the Bereaved
Email: NCMBereave@aol.com
http://www.griefwork.org/

Memory Tree of Lights – In Memory of Loved Ones Lost to Suicide
Email: founder@memorytrees.org
http://www.memorytrees.org/
Heartbeat – Grief Support Following Suicide
http://www.heartbeatsurvivorsaftersuicide.org/

Friends and Families of Suicides
http://www.friendsandfamiliesofsuicide.com/

1000 Deaths
http://www.1000deaths.com/

SAVE – Suicide Awareness Voices of Education
7317 Cahill Road, Suite 207
Minneapolis, MN 55439-2080
Phone: 952-946-7998
E-mail: save@save.org
http://www.save.org

Dealing with Traumatic Situations:

The International Society for Traumatic Stress Studies
60 Revere Drive, Suite 500
Northbrook, IL 60062
Phone: 847/480-9028
Fax: 847/480-9282
E-mail: istss@istss.org
http://www.istss.org

Association of Traumatic Stress Specialists
7338 Broad River Rd.
Irmo, South Carolina 29063
Phone: 803-781-0017
Fax: 803-781-3899
Email: tidwell@netside.com
http://www.atss-hq.com/index.cfm

International Critical Incident Stress Foundation, Inc.
http://www.icisf.org/

Gift from Within – Resource for survivors of trauma
16 Cobb Hill Rd.
Camden, Maine 04843
Phone: 207-236-8858
Fax: 207-236-2818
Email: JoyceB3955@aol.com
http://www.giftfromwithin.org/

The Child Advocate – Helping Children Cope with Disasters
http://childadvocate.net/disaster.htm

Managing Traumatic Stress
http://helping.apa.org/daily/traumaticstress.html

National Center for PTSD
http://www.ncptsd.org/